For
Daniel Pope
Happy investing, Dan!.

Ry Harding

BEAT THE MARKET THE EASY WAY!

BEAT THE MARKET THE EASY WAY!

*Surprising Seasonal Strategies
Double the Market's Performance!*

SY HARDING

Beat the Market the Easy Way!: Surprising Seasonal Strategies Double the Market's Performance!

Published by Wheatmark™
610 East Delano Street, Suite 104
Tucson, Arizona 85705 U.S.A.
www.wheatmark.com

International Standard Book Number: 978-1-58736-918-6
Library of Congress Control Number: 2007932473

To my wife,
Dale Stewart Harding

Also by Sy Harding

1999—*Riding the Bear—How to Prosper in the Coming Bear Market*

1988—Present—*Sy Harding's Street Smart Report* (investment newsletter)

1997—Present—*Street Smart Report Online* (investment web site)

Contents

Acknowledgements

I'd like to thank those whose contributions made this book possible;

My wife Dale, whose editorial ability guided me away from obtuse economic and market jargon, adding to the book's readability.

My daughter Patricia, whose encouragement pushed me forward, and whose accountant background contributed so much to the research and verification of the back-testing of data.

My editor at Wheatmark Publishing Inc., Hayley Love, for working so efficiently in pulling the book together so it could be published in a timely manner.

Those whose prior work is the foundation from which much subsequent market research has sprung; Richard D. Wyckoff, Edson Gould, Arthur Merrill, John Magee, Ned Davis, Norman Fosback, Yale Hirsch, Gerald Appel.

Those market analysts and practitioners who have shared research, thoughts, analysis, and information over the years; Ned Davis (Ned Davis Research Inc.), Peter Eliades (Stock Market Cycles), Jeff Hirsch (Stock Traders Almanac), Ike Iossif (Aegean Capital Group), Alan Newman (Crosscurrents), Robert Prechtor (Elliott Wave Theorist), Jim Schmidt (Timer Digest), Joe Shaefer (The Stanford Advisory Group), Carl Swenlin (Decisionpoint), and so many others.

The conventional view serves to protect us
from the painful job of thinking.
John Kenneth Galbraith.

Introduction

You're disappointed with your investment performance. Yet you have heard that the stock market is by far the best investing venue for building important wealth. You have heard that it's better than bonds, real estate, collectibles, or any of the other asset classes that occasionally come into favor for awhile. And it's true.

You have seen theoretical studies showing how even lower-tier workers can accumulate several $millions by the time they retire. They simply need to contribute the maximum allowed every year to their employer's 401K plan, or to an IRA. And theoretically those studies are also factual.

And yet other studies show that 80% of individual investors managing their own money lose money in the stock market over the long-term, or fail to match the performance they would have by simply leaving their money in the bank.

How can these opposite results both be factual?

Primarily because few individual investors understand how the stock market really works. Fewer still follow any type of proven investment strategy over the long term.

Even those realizing the importance of having a strategy tend not to follow one for long. As soon as their strategy falters—and no strategy is on top every year—they switch to whatever approach received the most publicity for good performance the previous year. Frequently that switch takes place just as the newly discovered strategy is due to falter. And so they wind up constantly switching strategies, which obviously is to have no long-term strategy at all.

Still others simply buy and hold. They wind up making good

gains in rising markets, and then give the gains back in the next market downturn.

So if you are a typical investor, odds are you're very disappointed with your investment performance over the long term. You see lists of the previous year's best performing stocks, sectors, and mutual funds, and wonder why you were unable to pick them before their performance took place. You hear this year of an investment strategy that worked extremely well last year, or over the last three years, and wonder why you didn't know about it three years ago, or even one year ago.

You did very well in the last half of the 1990s—but then the 2000-2002 bear market took your gains away.

Too often you bought when you should have sold, and sold when you should have bought. Other times you decided to buy and hold, and wound up holding while your chosen stock or mutual fund fell into a dark hole.

It shouldn't be that way. Investing is consistently profitable for professional investors and Wall Street institutions. Public investors can also make great gains in bull markets *and keep them;* and then make more gains in bear markets.

There are proven strategies that will accomplish that, *and with much less risk, effort, and stress than is involved in chasing hot tips and worrying about each week's hiccup in the market.*

But *first* you have to understand how the markets really work.

A survey by the non-profit *Securities Investor Protection Corporation* in 2001 revealed that 85% of U.S. individual investors were unable to pass a simple five question 'survival' quiz. SIPC Vice-President Robert O'Hara said, *"We have been at this for more than 50 years, and we see the same problem over and over again. Investors are enticed in during bull markets, and then don't know what to do when things turn sour later. People need to take the time to learn the basics about investing, and how to put them into practice."*

Most importantly you must learn how and why the stock market trades consistently in monthly and annual seasonal patterns. You must learn how often the market cycles longer term between bull and bear markets, and how you can avoid most of the declines with surprising ease.

By the time you finish this book, you will know all this and much more.

Even if you are a professional investor or money manager, you are going to be able to make much larger gains from bull markets *and keep them*. And you are going to add to those profits during bear markets.

For instance, you will learn a simple strategy that takes advantage of the market's annual seasonal patterns. Back-tested over the previous 50 years, and used in real-time over the last eight years, it more than doubled the performance of the S&P 500 and Nasdaq. Yet, it did so while taking only 50% of normal market risk. Most recently it allowed investors to make the big gains of the 1990s bull market, *keep those gains*, and then go on to make further gains in the devastating 2000-2002 bear market.

If you prefer a strategy that requires more activity, you will learn of a monthly trading strategy that Mark Hulbert of *Hulbert Financial Digest* fame, says had the best long-term performance on a risk-adjusted basis of all the strategies he has tracked over the last 20 years.

You will find this journey through the investment world, and the knowledge it provides, a fascinating trip that will forever change the way you approach investing.

After you have read this book, please help us get the word out to other investors, by word of mouth, via the Internet's chat rooms and blogs, and in your investment clubs. Please recommend this book to friends, family members, anyone you care about who would benefit from a superior, yet easy to understand, investment program.

BEAT THE MARKET THE EASY WAY!

Make gains in both bull and bear markets!

PART 1

Essential Facts You Need to Know First

You *must* learn how the markets work *before* you learn of the strategies I will provide.

Otherwise you will not understand why you need them, and will go on dreaming that you can win by following hot tips and the helter-skelter approach that has caused you problems in the past. You must not look on these strategies as just another 'idea', a tip that you might try for awhile.

You must understand *why* they work, and why the two most popular strategies used by 90% of public investors, 'chasing performance' and 'buy & hold', will *not* work—cannot work.

I will also show you that when investing their own money Wall Street institutions, mutual fund managers, hedge fund managers, brokerage firms, corporate insiders, and large individual investors do not use the strategies they recommend to public investors. Why is that?

Chapter 1

On Competing with Professionals!

In the introduction I promised that, like Wall Street institutions and professional investors, public investors can also make great profits in bull markets. Much more importantly, they can keep those profits, and even add to them with more gains in the subsequent bear markets. I will prove that to you beyond any doubt.

But first, you must imprint upon your mind a few important facts that are invariably forgotten once an investor gets caught up in the euphoria of an exciting bull market, or in the anxiety that prevails in a plunging bear market:

- The market does not move endlessly in one direction. Not to the upside, as many believe when they put hard-earned money in a mutual fund and expect it to just keep growing in value through the years. Not to the downside, as many believe after watching previous profits disappear in a painful bear market, and decide to "swear off the damned market for good".

- Serious corrections in individual stocks and sectors, and overall bear markets, are not rare events. The record ten-year long 1990s bull market misled many investors terribly in that regard. The fact is that the market cycles back and forth between rallies and corrections in the intermediate-term on average of every six months. It cycles between powerful bull markets and devastating bear markets on average of every three or four years.

It's not a surprising conclusion then that we need a strategy which at a minimum will put us on the right side of the market's major cycles in a fairly timely manner. Otherwise we will simply make good profits when the market is rising, and then give most of those profits back when the market next moves to the downside.

To break that pattern, among other requirements, you need to know when to accept Wall Street's buy recommendations, and when to avoid Wall Street's efforts to keep you buying long after the cycle has changed direction to the downside.

Developing a healthy skepticism regarding Wall Street's efforts to influence your thinking is one of the most important, yet most difficult, steps you must achieve to become a successful investor.

As Jeremy Grantham, founder of Grantham, Mayo, Van Otterloo and Co., which manages $140 billion for its clients, puts it, *"Investors need to be aware that everything they hear or read is always 90% dripping with bullish bias. It sells stocks, and for the record it sells books and magazines."*

Yes, Wall Street is bullish 90% of the time, regardless of whether it's a time to be buying, or a time to be selling. Therefore, 90% of what you hear or read in the media is always bullish no matter how ill-timed that might be, since the media obtains its information from its Wall Street 'contacts'.

In 2002, CNBC-TV had great fun looking back at how Wall Street firms had continued to rate stocks as buys most of the way down in the 2000-2002 bear market, even as those stocks lost 50% and more of their value. As CNBC-TV anchor Joe Kernen said at the time, *"For the most part brokerage firms only changed to sell recommendations long after the damage had been done."*

Looking back to discover that's how it worked in that bear market served mostly as entertainment. However, investors need to know that is how *always* works. Wall Street will rarely tell you when to sell in a timely manner.

- So, you must make sure you have sufficient knowledge of how the markets really work, so *you* will know when to sell.

- You must also have a strategy that works for part-time, non-professional, investors.

Few investors give the latter much thought. They assume they can simply attempt the same type of analysis professional money managers use to gauge which sector or which company will perform better than another.

Think about that. As someone whose specialized education, training, experience, and career may be in the field of accounting, electrical engineering, plumbing, law, medicine, sales, business management, or whatever, you are an expert in your own full-time profession. You realize it would be foolish for someone not trained in your profession to try to compete with you.

You know it would be irrational for a salesman to believe he could make extra money in the legal profession by spending his spare time reading university law journals, and watching court trials on TV. It would be equally unrealistic for an attorney to believe he could make extra money on weekends as a physician by simply reading medical journals and watching physicians discuss their techniques on TV. You would not entertain such a notion for a moment.

Yet most investors do not see it as the same situation when they try to compete in their spare time with professional money-managers and traders, by doing no more than reading financial publications, and listening to money managers discuss the market on TV.

You need to realize that managing assets using the methods of institutions and professionals is as complex a profession as any other. It requires in-depth knowledge of economic and market forces, specialized education, training, experience, the ability to analyze financial statements, evaluate corporate managements, project sales and earnings trends, and so on. It involves technical charting and analysis, and requires the support of data collection systems, information sources, contacts, and time.

Most individual investors realize they do not have the specialized education or experience to work professionally as a portfolio manager. Yet they commit their own hard-earned money to the belief that they can manage their investments by competing head to head with the professionals in their spare time. It is obviously to Wall Street's advantage to have them believe that is true.

Thomas Kostigen, a market analyst and columnist with MarketWatch puts it very bluntly. *"Investment professionals profit off the backs of the naïve investing public. Investors willingly step onto the Wall Street game field and think they can compete with the pros, highly trained and highly skilled professionals who live and breathe the market, and they play hardball. Dilettante investors watch the game. It looks easy so they think they can play too. Only they play without training or equipment, and they get hurt."*

Unfortunately, the lack of training and equipment leads to the biggest problems and mistakes of most investors.

You may recognize some of your own problems in the following chapters.

Chapter 2

Tips, Touts, & Chasing Performance

ACTING ON TIPS

Hampered by limited time, experience, and information, the market-timing and stock-picking of many investors comes down to investing based on 'tips'. They accept the stock or mutual fund recommendations of well-meaning friends, and even strangers in chat rooms, or blogs, on the Internet. They don't seem to realize that those people also do not have the time or facilities for research, and at best are just passing along tips received elsewhere. At worst, gullible investors may even be victimized by the deliberate scams that permeate the Internet.

Many a crooked stock promoter has been caught after forming a phony company, listing its stock in the 'pink sheets', and hiring people to spread positive stories about it in chat room discussions. As the Securities & Exchange Commission warns investors, many more remain in business than are caught.

It's also quite a game for 'clever' traders and speculators to surf the edge of legality by buying shares in a legitimate company, and then arranging for employees, friends, and relatives to swarm into chat rooms and blogs with glowing assessments of it. That often gets a stock moving. That initial move provides the other participants in the chat room with convincing evidence of the 'accuracy' of the tip, and they innocently also begin spreading the word. Their additional publicity and remarks bring still more buying. The smiling speculator, and his co-conspirators, aware that the recommendation had no real basis in fact, happily sell into the strength, and move onto another stock.

Of the situation, Arthur Levitt, chairman of the Securities & Exchange Commission at the time, had this to say in 1999; *"Chat rooms and bulletin boards have increasingly become a source of information, and misinformation, for many investors. Supporters refer to them as a high-tech version of morning gossip, or advice exchanged around the water cooler. But at least you know your co-workers at the water cooler well enough to make a judgment regarding the probable quality of their advice. That just isn't true on the Internet, and I hope investors will come to recognize that. I wonder how many chat room participants realize that if someone is waxing poetic about a certain stock, that person could well be being paid to do it."*

Individual investors also tend to consider the stock tips offered by money managers being interviewed on TV or in magazines as valid research for their own situations. Yet each of those professionals has a different strategy and approach.

Therefore over time an investor will wind up with a portfolio of which a few stocks were chosen based on a 'bottoms-up' approach, a few following a 'tops-down' strategy, a few that were based on perhaps the 'Dogs of the Dow' strategy, or a seasonal strategy, some based on their fundamentals, others on technical 'breakouts'.

Chances are the investor will soon not even remember where he got the tip, or why he owns the various stocks that are in his portfolio.

Among other problems, the tip is received by hundreds of thousands of TV viewers or magazine readers at the same time, and has probably already been promoted to other audiences, as the Wall Street manager makes the rounds of the financial shows. That is hardly a means of getting in on a good buying opportunity before the 'crowd' catches on.

In fact, professional traders often take advantage of the gullibility of individual investors in accepting such tips.

James Cramer of CNBC's *Mad Money* fame, tells the story of how, in his previous career as a hedge fund manager, he watched for announcements of upcoming interviews on TV financial shows.

Prior to a guest's appearance he would check out the person's most recent interviews elsewhere, note their favorite stocks, and buy them a few hours before the interview. He expected those would be the stocks the guest would be touting again.

Cramer said he would usually get a quick pop in the stocks the day of the guest's appearance, and the following day. Then, knowing the rally in the stock price would probably be temporary, he would sell, making small but frequent profits. Most often, within a few days the stock would drop back to its level prior to the interview.

That should not be surprising. The pop in the stock's price was not due to a change in the company's value, such as might be expected after a better earnings report, or announcement of a new product. It was due only to a temporary surge in demand created by its mention on the TV show.

Meanwhile, even when a tip is a good tip, there is no hope of receiving the equally important second half of successful investing. That is, being told when to sell—either to take the profit, or to cut a loss before it becomes larger.

Yet another mistake of investors, lacking the time or information to engage in actual research, is:

CHASING PERFORMANCE.

Another favorite approach of non-professional investors is to buy the stocks and mutual funds that receive publicity for having been the previous year's big winners. It's known as 'chasing performance', investing in a holding *after* it has made great gains.

How great a strategy is that, even on its surface, considering that the most obvious rule for successful investing is to buy *low* and sell high? And indeed, studies have shown that a list of the previous year's *losers* is more likely to be fertile ground for finding the following year's winners, as they are more likely to be oversold and due for a reversal to the upside.

Yet as each year draws to a close, millions of investors begin their annual routine of using screening tools on the Internet, and reviewing 'Top 25 Mutual Funds' lists in magazines, to find out which funds were the top performers the previous year, or for the previous three years.

How popular is the strategy? *The Investment Company Institute* says that 88% of mutual fund buyers cite a fund's *previous* performance as the primary reason they choose one fund over another.

Does it work?

Not according to highly respected research company Morningstar Inc. It rates mutual funds based largely on their past performance, giving those with the highest ranking five stars, the next best four stars, and so forth.

Money flows show that each year investors switch money out of the poorly ranked funds into the top-ranked funds. Meanwhile, the top-ranked funds are usually those that happened to be in the hottest sectors in the previous measuring period; technology, the financial sector, small-cap sector, emerging markets, or whatever.

John Rekenthaler, Morningstar's vice-president of research, says that almost always *"investors piling into the hottest funds of the previous period will be sorry, since the lower ranked funds tend to be the winners over the next three-year period"*.

The following table is courtesy of Morningstar Inc. It shows the performance of the top-30 funds in each four-year period from 1976—2002, and how their performance then declined sharply in the following four-year period (with a different group of funds repeatedly taking over the top ranking).

Performance of Mutual Funds after ranking in Top 30 for four-year performance. Jan. 1976—Dec. 2002.		
	Annualized Return 1976—1980	***Subsequent* Annualized Return 1981—1985**
Top 30 Funds 1976—1980	34.3%	9.9%
Average of all funds	15.8%	7.7%
S&P 500 Index	14.0%	12.2%

Previous Top-30 having failed a new group is next top-30.	Annualized Return 1981—1985	Subsequent Annualized Return 1986—1990
Top 30 Funds 1981—1985	21.7%	9.7%
Average of all funds	10.9%	8.0%
S&P 500 Index	14.7%	11.5%
Previous Top-30 having failed a new group is next top-30.	Annualized Return 1986—1990	Subsequent Annualized Return 1991—1995
Top 30 Funds 1986—1990	14.9%	10.1%
Average of all funds	8.1%	8.9%
S&P 500 Index	13.2%	10.8%
Previous Top-30 having failed a new group is next top-30.	Annualized Return 1991—1995	Subsequent Annualized Return 1996—2000
Top 30 Funds 1991—1995	39.8%	2.1%
Average of all funds	16.3%	4.7%
S&P 500 Index	16.6%	6.9%
Previous Top-30 having failed a new group is next top-30.	Annualized Return 1996—2000	Subsequent Annualized Return 2001—2002
Top 30 Funds 1996—2000	31.0%	- 22.8%
Average of all funds	15.2%	- 17.2%
S&P 500 Index	18.3%	- 17.2%
Information courtesy of: Morningstar Inc.		

The S&P 500 is the benchmark against which investment performance is measured. The table makes it clear that the *average* mutual fund manager fails to match the performance of the S&P 500 in *any* period.

It makes it equally clear that of those that manage to have four years in which they do outperform the market, even the *best* 30 of those funds tend to significantly under-perform the S&P 500 in the next four-year cycle. Whatever produced their four years of great performance was apparently not tied to long-term abilities or skills, but to some other shorter-term factor.

The work of independent research firm Dalbar Inc. also finds that chasing performance is a fool's game.

Dalbar periodically publishes a study titled 'The Quantitative Analysis of Investor Behavior'. The study compares the average performance of mutual funds to the performance of the investors who invest in them. The results are amazing, and you need to give them considerable thought.

For instance, Dalbar's 2003 study showed that from 1984—2002 the average annual return of the S&P 500 was 12.2%, while the average annual return of mutual funds was only 9.3%. Even more revealing, the average annual return of investors who invested in those funds was only 2.6%.

What were investors doing wrong that they were making so much less than the mutual funds they were investing in? According to Dalbar Inc., which analyzed the timing of money flows into and out of the funds as part of its research, the vast majority were "chasing the latest hot performance". They were moving into a fund *after* it had great performance, then bailing out of it when it didn't perform as well in the subsequent period, to switch yet again to one that did have exceptional performance in the previous period. Buying high and selling low.

You might expect fixed-income investors, those looking for income rather than capital gains, to be more disciplined, less likely to jump from fund to fund.

But Dalbar's 2006 report showed that bond investors tend to follow the same pattern. Over the 20-year period from 1986—2005, the average annual return of bond investors was just 1.8%, while the Long-Term Government Bond Index had an average annual return of 9.7%. It was again a case of investors looking back to see which type of bond fund provided the best return in the previous period relative to the one they were in, and switching into it. They usually did so just in time for that type of fund to begin under-performing, while the one they exited began a period of outstanding performance.

- **It's important to learn *this* from the Morningstar and Dalbar studies:** The investment performance you obtain from a mutual fund depends much more on your own actions than on the ability of the fund manager.

About now, having read all of a dozen or so pages of information, you're probably saying, "So okay, I obviously need a different approach. I'm guilty of sometimes following tips, often chasing performance, and not really having a defined long-term strategy. You say you'll tell us of strategies that will beat the performance of professional managers without the need for their knowledge and expertise. So tell us!"

Patience! You don't want just another hot tip.

This time you're going to first learn how the markets work. You're going to learn why most of what you are told by Wall Street serves their purposes, not yours.

Otherwise, you will have no new understanding. You will follow the proven strategies I am going to tell you about only until you get a hot tip that sounds better, or until Wall Street tells you again that there is only one way to invest successfully.

So be patient, and learn.

Next learn the truth about what Wall Street tells you is the only way for investors to invest—buy & hold. That is, buy what they sell you and hold it through whatever comes along.

Chapter 3

The Truth About Buy & Hold Investing

Wall Street will tell you that the answer to your investing problems is to simply buy and hold. Choose a good stock or mutual fund and hold it for the very long term, through whatever comes along.

The Dalbar Inc. study noted in the previous chapter might also lead you in that direction. It shows that on a buy and hold basis the average mutual fund outperforms individual investors in the funds by wide margins because the investors jump from fund to fund. But the problem is not that they don't buy and hold, but that they don't know when to buy, or when to sell. So they buy high, after a fund has performed, and bail out after it has declined.

So let's continue. It is *most* important that you know and understand the truth about buy and hold. Too often even those investors who do not consider themselves to be buy & hold investors will see their holdings run into problems and not know what to do. So they do nothing, telling themselves "Well, I'll just hold on, buy & hold is supposed to be the way to go anyway."

Buy & hold's biggest problem is obviously that the market does not move in one direction. It has ups and downs.

- So anyone staying fully invested all the time is *guaranteed* to periodically suffer losses, sometimes serious losses from which recovery may take many years.

It's obviously a problem even for professional money managers. They remain fully invested all the time, although not in the same ock or mutual fund. They try to lessen the effect of periodic market declines through risk management, and switching to 'defensive' stocks or sectors. *It doesn't work.*

- The majority of money managers and mutual funds do not even match, let alone outperform, the S&P 500 over the long term. In fact, on average they miss the benchmark by quite a wide margin.

Don't believe it?

Recall that Dalbar Inc. study again, of mutual funds from 1984-2002. It showed that the average annual return of mutual funds was 9.3%. As I noted in the previous chapter, that was infinitely better than the 2.6% average annual return of the investors in the funds (who kept jumping in and out with the poorest of timing). However, the S&P 500 had an average annual gain of 12.2% during the period. The funds did not come close to matching the market's performance.

How substantial is the difference between the S&P 500's average annual return of 12.2% and the 9.3% average annual return of mutual funds? Very substantial. An annual return of 12.2% compounded over a 20-year period would turn $100,000 into $999,655. An average annual return of 9.3% would turn that same $100,000 into only $592,111.

Yes, although professional managers significantly outperform non-professional investors, most professionals also fail to even match the market's performance. That shows how difficult it is (and the value of the strategies I will show you that double and triple the long-term performance of the market).

Let's look at more evidence of how difficult it is to win the game that Wall Street and investors play.

- A study by First Quadrant L.P. shows that on average, over *any* 20-year period 78% of mutual funds fail to even *match* the performance of the S&P 500.

The record would actually be worse if it were not for a nasty little game mutual fund companies use to hide their poorest performing funds. They simply close them down, or fold them into a more successful fund, their poor performance disappearing from the records forever.

In 1997 the *Journal of Finance* published a comprehensive study of mutual funds for the period from 1962—1993. The study was conducted by Mark Carhart, managing director at Goldman Sachs Asset Management at the time. In the study Carhart states that *"by 1993 fully one-third of all the mutual funds of the period had disappeared."*

That is understandable. There were numerous opportunities between 1962 and 1993 for mutual funds to perform poorly, for a mutual fund company to want to hide that performance by merging their worst funds into their better funds. The period included no fewer than seven bear markets, one on average of every 4.4 years, with the declines averaging 30.4%.

How important are a fund's operating expenses?

Wall Street and the financial media try to pour a little fog over the situation. They tell investors their main problem in not obtaining satisfactory performance from mutual funds is that they don't pay enough attention to a fund's operating expenses. They point out that the fees a fund charges for operating the fund come directly out of the fund's performance. So a fund that has to charge 1.5% fees to cover expenses will not perform as well as a fund with fees of only 0.9% per share. And naïve investors believe that is an important consideration.

Listen to me! Of all places, investing your hard-earned money is not an area where the 'contract' should necessarily go to the lowest cost bidder. Performance *after* costs is all that matters. An investor should be looking for a fund with exceptional management as most likely to provide exceptional performance. And if a management team's ability is exceptional, an investor should expect it to command higher salaries, and to be paying more for its information than a bare bones operation.

No, the problem for mutual funds is not that one fund has fractionally higher operating costs than another. The problem is that the S&P 500 averages a 12.2% annual return over the long term, while mutual funds average only 9.3% (and investors in the funds average only 2.6%).

Even so, the biggest problem for investors is obviously in that number of 2.6%. It shows that even *if* mutual funds could assure you of beating the market over the long-term, trying to buy and hold them would not work for most investors. Investors prove they are unable to hold a mutual fund even when it's making gains, if the gains are not as large as those of the best performing funds of the previous year, or previous three years. Virtually none are able to hold through a bear market, when their mutual fund is losing as much as 30% to 50% of its value.

- Yet, for the buy & hold strategy to succeed you would have to not only hold through the bear market, but would have to continue to hold until the market returns to its previous level.

That just would not happen. Statistics make it clear that by far the majority of investors, including those who intended to be buy and hold investors, bail out near bear market lows. They then don't get back in until the next bull market has been underway long enough to convince them that everything is okay again.

- It is best to recognize that would probably be your result *before* you decide to be a buy and hold investor, rather than after the damage is done.

Buy and hold is essentially a strategy in theory only. Almost no one could follow it for the long-term.

However, it is even a badly flawed theory.

For instance, Wall Street firms advise individual investors to "Have a long-term outlook. Buy good stocks or mutual funds and hold them through whatever comes along. Do not try to time the market."

But, oh—the problems!

To begin with—what *is* a good stock?

Stocks thought to be good stocks come in two flavors.

In bull markets, when all stocks seem to be going up and investors are full of confidence, the stocks of new companies, with new products or services related to what is expected to be "the next big thing", are thought to be the good stocks that will last forever. Hopefully they will turn out to be the next eBay, or Google, or the next evolution in retailing, perhaps the next Home Depot or Best Buy.

At other times, when investors are made nervous by a deterioration in economic or other conditions, their perception of what is a good stock changes. The stocks of large, proven companies that have been around through several boom and bust economic periods, and are respected as solid companies, a Coca-Cola, General Electric, Merck, Microsoft, or Procter & Gamble, are thought to be the good stocks.

However, the truth is there are no 'good' stocks in either category that will protect one from devastating losses in a serious market correction or bear market. Those that are thought to be good stocks for awhile, almost always sooner or later become disasters looking for complacent investors to land on.

An entire book could be filled with the history of thousands of such stocks thought at the time to be 'forever' stocks that could be bought and held for decades, and even passed on to the next generation. Yet a list of those whose price actually held up for even five to ten years would hardly fill a postcard.

You might laugh and think it's irrelevant when I tell you that 100 years ago Distilling & Cattle Feeding Inc., American Cotton Oil Company, and U.S. Leather Inc., were thought by our great-grandfathers to be such solid and important companies that their stocks were safe 'buy and hold forever' stocks. They were even important components of the Dow Jones Industrial Average, as were American Beet Sugar, and Baldwin Locomotive.

In the next generation our grandparents got excited about companies like Studebaker, Packard, Fox Theaters, North American Aviation, Marconi, thinking their stocks were 'forever' stocks.

After the development of the internal combustion engine in the early 1900s, more than 2,000 companies were launched worldwide to produce automobiles, certainly a big new thing destined to last forever. But only a handful of the companies launched to participate in that next big thing survived after they ran through the start-up money provided by their investors.

The introduction of electricity brought an endless array of new electrical products for homes and businesses; electric lamps, toasters, electric irons, radios. *Thousands* of exciting new companies popped up all over the place to produce them, and for investors to get excited about, Servel refrigerators, Excel electric cookers, Rotorex electric irons, Warner Vacuum cleaners. Alas, few survived.

Yes, it's funny now to think that our forefathers could not see that times would continue to change, that they did not realize that as exciting and profitable as new products were in their time, they were destined to be overtaken by newer 'new things', or newer versions of old things.

They were not being dumb. In each period investors were only doing what investors have always done, which is to hope they can get in on the ground floor of the next new technological marvel.

And the interesting thing is that they often do wind up with great stocks that work well for them, *if they sell them soon enough to pocket the profits.* However, the early pioneering companies even in technologies that survived, as railroads, automobiles, electrical products, gasoline-powered products, aircraft, television, computers, the Internet, etc., certainly have, seldom survived as strong stocks once competitors came along with improvements, better methods of manufacturing, distribution, advertising, or whatever.

Admiral, Belmont, Bendix, Capehart, Crosley, DuMont, Emerson, Hallicrafters, Magnavox, Philco, Stromberg-Carlson, Curtiss Wright, Polaroid, General Transistor, Xerox, ComSat, Itek, Burroughs, Mohawk Data, Control Data. Oh, the excitement over those stocks when they were launched and for a few years after. It was the same thing with the great early computer stocks like Altair, Atari, Commodore, Kaypro, Osborne, Tandy, Wang Laboratories, and then the *next* generation of computer manufacturers like AST, Compaq, Gateway. Great companies, with exciting new products and early success. Surely buy and hold forever stocks—Not.

In 1999, 'E-tailer' internet stocks (on-line retailers) were thought by the current generation of investors to be 'forever' stocks. Talk about an investor's dream of getting in on the ground floor of 'the next big thing'.

But we know what happened. The Internet was certainly here to stay, spawning several thousand innovative new companies. They captured the imaginations of a new generation of investors, who threw many billions of dollars into their stocks. Fueled by so much money, they soared like Roman candles. But also like Roman candles, they soon sputtered and plunged to the ground, losing anywhere from 60% to 100% of their previous value. More than 500 of the exciting Internet companies introduced just in 1998 and 1999 totally disappeared into bankruptcy within three years of their launchings. Eight years later, the stocks of even those that did survive and thrived, the likes of Yahoo, Ameritrade, and Amazon. com, are still 50% to 75% below their 1999 prices.

Telecom, fiberoptics, automation, biotechnology, data storage, and other high-tech innovations of the late 1990s also attracted hundreds of $billions of investor assets. All of them produced huge profits for early investors *if they sold in time*. However, as always happens in bear markets, all crashed and burned in the 2000-2002 bear market.

The following table shows what happened to even those that had been considered the *best of the best in* 2000. They are still substantial companies. But were they 'good stocks', as in Wall Street's advice to simply buy good stocks and hold them through whatever comes along?

The table shows their prices on March 27, 2000, compared to their prices at the bear market low, less than three years later, *and more than seven years later*, in May, 2007. Even though a new bull market began in 2002, the stocks were still well below their levels at the bull market top in 2000.

They were, and are, good companies. But their stocks simply became overvalued in the 1990s bull market, and have corrected back to normal valuations.

Company	Mar. 27, 2000	2002 Low	Decline	May, 2007	Still down
Applied Materials	57.44	10.35	- 82%	19.10	- 66%
Cisco Systems	80.06	8.60	- 89%	26.39	- 67%
Dell Computer	57.87	22.61	-61%	25.95	- 55%
Intel	60.09	13.22	-78%	22.90	- 62%
JDS Uniphase	128.75	1.62	- 99%	13.12	- 90%
Microsoft	52.03	21.41	- 59%	30.81	- 41%
Oracle	44.22	7.32	- 83%	19.36	- 56%
Qualcom	74.47	11.87	- 84%	45.84	- 38%
Sirius Satellite Radio	53.06	0.52	- 99%	2.78	- 94%
Sun Microsystems	52.50	2.42	- 95%	5.38	- 89%
Yahoo	100.37	4.50	-95%	28.80	- 71%
Average			- 84%		- 60%

Compounding the problem, investors were so enamored of the stocks that they kept buying more all the way down in the bear market, on the popular but erroneous theory that if a company was a great stock at $65 a share, it must be a great bargain at $50, and even more so at $25.

So as in previous generations, even the best of 'the next big thing' companies did not turn out to be stocks that could be held 'through whatever comes along'.

How about those large, solid, conservative 'defensive' stocks?

It's even more disappointing to those trusting buy & hold advice, that the stocks of conservative companies, which have been around through several boom and bust economic periods, and are highly respected as solid companies, repeatedly prove they also are not buy and 'hold through whatever comes' along stocks.

Put them under the mattress and forget about them stocks like AT&T, Coca-Cola, General Electric, Ford, General Motors, IBM, Proctor & Gamble, Merck, WalMart, even Microsoft and Intel, have been some of the worst stocks to own in recent years (and were in numerous previous periods).

Contrary to Wall Street's assurances, they were unable to avoid the severe losses of the 2000-2002 bear market. And even seven years after *their* 1999 bull market tops most remain more than 30% below those levels. Some will probably never recover to their over-valued 1999 levels.

The following table shows a sampling of stocks considered by Wall Street in 1999 to be conservative, safe, 'defensive' stocks. The table shows their 1999-2000 bull market high, their subsequent bear market lows, and their prices more than seven years later, in May, 2007, *even after the next bull market had been underway for five years.*

Company	Bull Market Top	2002 Low	Decline	May 2007	Still down
Alcoa	43.62	17.62	- 60%	39.08	- 10%
Bristol Myers	73.93	20.55	- 72%	29.95	- 59%
CitiGroup	58.87	26.73	- 54%	54.84	- 7%
Coca-Cola	66.87	26.81	- 60%	51.68	- 23%
Disney	43.00	13.77	- 68%	36.44	- 15%
DuPont	64.62	34.10	- 47%	51.99	- 20%
Fannie Mae	87.81	59.54	- 32%	62.91	- 28%
General Electric	59.87	22.00	- 63%	37.10	- 38%
General Motors	93.37	31.01	- 67%	31.18	- 67%
Home Depot	68.50	20.53	- 70%	38.49	- 44%
IBM	137.87	56.60	- 59%	106.58	- 23%
Kodak	79.75	25.87	- 67%	24.97	- 69%
Merck	94.87	39.05	- 57%	53.79	- 43%
WalMart	69.31	44.00	-37%	46.62	- 33%
Average			- 59%		- 34%

You probably remember why you were told these best of the best, conservative blue chip stocks would hold up well in any correction or bear market.

The 'stories' are always similar, designed to make you think you can choose stocks that will not be affected by economic slowdowns or bear markets.

Some would hold up because no matter what happened to the economy or stock market, "people will still have to eat", or "people will still have to take their medicines", or "in bad economic times folks will more than ever need the discount and do-it-yourself outlets like WalMart and Home Depot, and credit card providers like CitiGroup".

- Yet if you had formed a portfolio of these blue chip stocks near their exciting top in 2000, you would have had a loss averaging a huge 59% by the time the bear market ended in 2002. *Seven years* after you bought them they would still be down an average of 34%. And these were not high risk, or even normal risk stocks, but highly recommended blue chips.

Unlike many of the Internet, telecom, fiberoptics, and other high-tech stocks, these blue chip companies did at least survive. But plunging so dramatically in the bear market, and still down significantly seven years after their tops in 2000, they were hardly the 'safe haven' buy and hold stocks they were touted to be.

Don't tell me it's unfair to include some of them because they ran into unexpected problems. I realize that General Motors ran into all kinds of grief from foreign competition, and its underfunded pension plans; that Merck ran into lawsuits surrounding its Vioxx drug; that in spite of a booming real estate market, mortgage provider Fannie Mae was hit by reports of accounting problems.

That only reinforces what I am saying, that there are almost no buy & hold stocks, no 'defensive' stocks. They are each periodically hit with individual problems of their own, and are *all* affected by bear markets.

- The thing of it is that consumers *will* still have to eat and take their medicines, and so will have to continue to buy the products of those companies. However, *investors* will not have to continue to value the stocks of those companies at the extremes of overvaluation seen at the previous market top.

That is, a company's earnings may remain the same or even rise. But in the euphoria of a bull market investors may be willing to pay

30 times those earnings for its stock, while in the throes of a bear market they will pay only 10 times earnings for the same stock. So even though a company's sales and profits may continue to rise, its stock price will still plunge.

So, the first problem with advice to simply buy 'good stocks' and hold them through whatever market or economic problems come along, is; how on earth can an investor hope to identify such a stock, let alone a diversified portfolio of them through the years, when even Wall Street firms are unable to do so?

There are roughly 10,000 stocks available, and a good 'story' is available about most of them. Consequently, there is an endless supply of stocks that can be touted as 'good stocks', and are—when the market is going up.

They may be companies that will get investors in on the ground floor of the next big thing. They may be solid conservative companies. But the evidence of how few, if any, are suitable to be held through whatever comes along is quite dismal.

Even so, the difficulty of picking companies that will not be dragged down in market declines is but one problem with the myth of buy and hold investing.

Another is that even the basic supporting argument for buy and hold investing is false, which is that "The market always comes back!"

WHAT MARKET ALWAYS COMES BACK?

The phrase "The market always comes back" is a powerful confidence builder for investors. It says we don't have to be concerned about risk, or market downturns. Even if a nasty bear market comes along, even if it takes our good stocks down with it, there is no need for concern. As long as we have a long-term outlook, 'the market always comes back'.

The phrase is a great selling tool for Wall Street. There's never a need to wait for better market conditions. Just invest any time, and let time take care of it.

But wait a minute. Aren't there a couple of serious problems with the theory?

For instance, how long are you willing to wait for the market to come back, with your investments seriously underwater?

After the stock market top in 1929 it was twenty-six years before the market finally returned to its level of 1929. A 40-year old investor in 1929 was 66 years old, and probably retired by 1955, when he finally saw the market back to its level of 1929. *Some investors would have died while waiting.*

Just 11 years later, in 1966, the DJIA reached another new high. It touched the level of 1,000 for the first time ever. It then plunged 35%, and it was 16 years later, 1981, before the DJIA finally reached 1,000 again and began to exceed that level.

Between the two periods that was a total of 42 years out of 70 that buy and hold investors would have been waiting for the market to 'come back'.

Was that a phenomenon of the old days that won't be seen again? No.

Current investors who bought and held in 1999 and 2000 can only be wondering how long it will take for *their* holdings to get back to 1999 levels. By early 2007 it had already been seven years.

It was late 2006 before the 30-stock Dow returned to its level achieved at the 2000 market peak. It was May, 2007 before the S&P 500 returned to its level of early 2000.

More indicative of where the average investors' buy & hold portfolio would be, by May, 2007 the Nasdaq, favorite playing field of public investors in 1999, was still 50% *below* its peak of 7 years earlier. Obviously the majority of 'buy & hold' investors' portfolios were not close to having 'come back', even seven years after the 2000 market top.

No wonder buy & hold investing is ridiculed by knowledgeable investors.

- *However,* for those able to ignore Wall Street's advice to 'buy & hold', who followed a strategy that called for taking profits near market tops, there were tremendous profit opportunities.

For example, as shown in the following chart of the stock market from 1922—1939; after the 1929-32 bear market loss of 86%, although the DJIA did not get back to its 1929 level for 26 years, it did produce a super 370% gain from its 1932 low to its 1937 high.

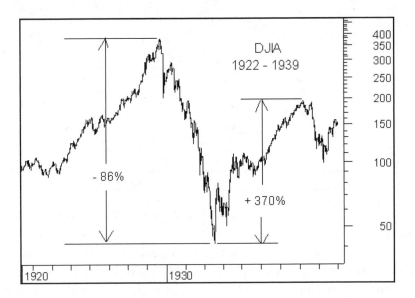

But only those who exited before the 1929 crash began, keeping their profits from the 1920s bull market, had the cash in 1932 to take advantage of that next bull market.

As shown in the next chart, it was a similar situation for buy and hold investors in the 16-year period that began in 1966.

The Dow reached a new high, at 1000, in 1966. From that point it plunged 35%, and it was 16 years later, in 1982, before the Dow finally rose above 1000 and kept rising.

It was a devastating period for buy and hold investors who bought in 1965 or 1966. They saw their portfolios underwater for the next 16 years, down as much as 45%, as they waited for the market 'to come back'.

But once again, it was a wonderful period for 'market-timers' to make significant profits from both the upside and the downside, as the market continued to cycle between substantial bull and

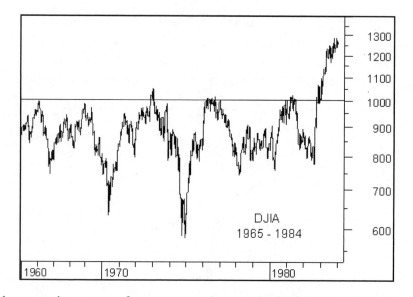

bear markets every few years, each one of which lasted for several years.

It can be reasonably assumed that each new market decline convinced more buy and hold investors to give up on the strategy, and to do so with the worst of timing, by bailing out in disgust near one of the lows.

More recent periods of devastation for those waiting for a market to 'come back'.

In the late 1980s Japan was an exciting market, and was therefore a favorite area for investors around the world, including U.S. investors.

However, in 1989 the Japanese Nikkei reached 38,915 and then topped out. It plunged 80% over the next 14 years.

Even today, in 2007, in spite of numerous cyclical bull markets that lasted several years, the Japanese market remains 55% below its 1989 peak.

If there were any buy and hold investors who actually held through the 14-year decline (of course there were not), will they live long enough to see that market 'come back'? It's already been 18 years, and it has not recovered even half of its losses.

However, for anyone who took their profits near the top in

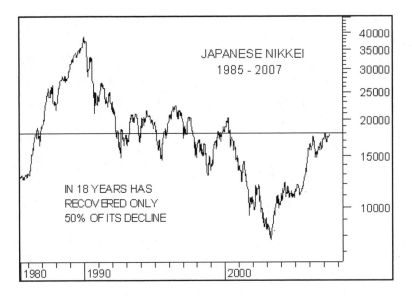

JAPANESE NIKKEI
1985 - 2007

IN 18 YEARS HAS
RECOVERED ONLY
50% OF ITS DECLINE

1989, look at all those opportunities to make gains in substantial two and three-year bull markets, even as the Nikkei continued to decline over the long-term.

It's a similar situation in the U.S. with the Nasdaq.

In March of 2000, the Nasdaq, the favorite investment area for U.S. investors in the 1990s bull market, hit a high of 5,132. In the 2000-2002 bear market that followed, it plunged to 1,114, a loss of 78%.

Seven years after its peak, in spite of the new bull market that began in 2002, it is still 50% below its level at its 2000 top. How many more years will investors have to wait for *it* to 'come back'?

The problem with Wall Street's claim that 'the market always comes back, so just take a long-term view', is obvious. That long-term view may need to be very long indeed.

Yet there are even more problems with buy and hold investing;

When the market does finally come back, it's not the same market that went away.

That may seem like a strange statement. However, the claim that the market always comes back is based on the fact that the Dow, S&P 500, and Nasdaq *indexes* always eventually get back to

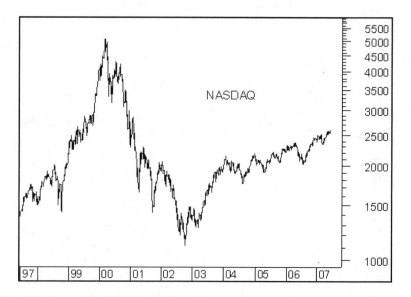

their previous highs (even though it may take fifteen to twenty-five years), and then go on to make new highs.

However the stocks that make up those indexes are changed so often that it makes even the eventual comeback of the indexes meaningless as far as whether an investor's portfolio will come back.

For instance, 23% of the stocks that were in the DJIA in 1999 were no longer in that index by 2004, just five years later. They were replaced a few at a time by stocks of newer, stronger companies that were more representative of the changing economy. Chevron, Goodyear Tire, Union Carbide and Sears Roebuck were replaced by Microsoft, Intel, SBC Communications and Home Depot. AT&T was replaced by Verizon. Eastman Kodak was replaced by Pfizer. International Paper was replaced by AIG Group.

- So what does it really mean to investors that were in the stocks of the 'old' index in 1999, that by 2007 the 'new' index had come back up to the level of the 1999 peak reached by the 'old' index?

It's been the same for more than a hundred years, since the Dow Jones Industrial Average was first developed (in 1896) to contain the stocks that most represented the overall U.S. economy at the time. I hope no one is still waiting for Distilling & Cattle Feeding Inc., or U.S. Leather Inc. to come back. As mentioned earlier, they were once components of the DJIA, as in later periods were American Cotton Oil, Baldwin Locomotive, and Victor Talking Machines Inc. As time passed and other industries became more representative of the nation's economy, each was replaced, by names like Nash Motors, Mack Trucks, Remington Typewriter, Woolworth, and dozens of others, now also forgotten, but once among the 30 stocks that made up the DJIA, and once prominent in investors' portfolios.

It has been the same with the newer stock indexes, like the S&P 500, introduced in 1957, the NASDAQ, introduced in 1971, and the NASDAQ 100, introduced in 1985.

- Just since early 1999, *in only seven years*, there have been 109 changes in the stocks that comprise the Nasdaq 100, an index that only contains 100 stocks.

The point is, even if we ignore how long it may take for 'the market' to come back, what does it really mean to say the market always comes back, if the stocks that previously made up the indexes fell out of favor and have been replaced with stronger stocks? Meanwhile, many of the previously popular stocks, which investors really need to come back if their portfolios are to come back, have been dropped from the index, and in some cases no longer even exist?

You have to wonder which currently strong stocks won't be in the indexes the next time the market declines and investors wait for *them* to 'come back'.

BUY AND HOLD ALSO MISSES OUT
ON OTHER OPPORTUNITIES.

While buy and hold investors are holding stocks as they decline in one market, great opportunities for profits are being missed elsewhere, in markets that are in new bull markets.

For instance, an investor who bought into the Japanese market in 1989 and held on through its subsequent 14-year bear market, missed out on the fabulous 1990s U.S. bull market. Those who held onto their tech stocks through the 2000-2002 bear market in the U.S., waiting for them to come back some day, missed out on the super new bull market in gold stocks which began in 2000.

And so it goes every time.

Buy and hold investing, while the most widely touted strategy for individual investors, is actually a sham, a farce, and a disaster waiting to land on trusting investors who don't bother to learn the truth.

To recap what we've learned about buy and hold as an investment strategy;

- Buy and hold investing is not a viable strategy because it is impossible to simply "pick good stocks and hold them long-term" since virtually all stocks are affected negatively by serious corrections and bear markets.

- The myth of buy and hold investing cannot even be supported by the promise that "the market always comes back", because it can take decades for even the market indexes to come back.

- And when the indexes do eventually come back, supposedly proving that the market has come back, they have undergone changes to include the newest strong companies, and so do not represent the same market that went away.

- Those holding their portfolio through a serious correction or bear market are usually missing out on opportunities they could be taking advantage of elsewhere, had they been willing to take their profits and move on.

Readers: "Okay then. So now you've convinced us that Wall Street is wrong when it tells us to buy and hold. We're more than willing to take profits by selling near tops. So tell us how to do that. What are those simple market-beating strategies?

Not so fast. Patience.

You still have not learned enough about how the markets work.

You will not follow any strategy if you remain susceptible to the suggestions and propaganda of the Wall Street forces that are lined up against you.

Next you are going to learn what Wall Street does with its own money.

Chapter 4

What Does Wall Street Do with Its Own Money?

The large and famous investors who made fortunes in 'the old days' and kept them, the likes of Joseph P. Kennedy, Bernard Baruch, Walter Chrysler, E.H. Harriman, J.P. Morgan, etc., were certainly not buy and hold investors. Not only did they not even try to buy 'good' stocks and hold them through the declines, they sold 'good' stocks short and made further fortunes from the market's declines. They were market-timers!

As I clearly showed in *Riding the Bear,* not only were they market-timers, they were market-manipulators. They repeatedly used false publicity and other tricks to entice public investors to buy more at tops, when the manipulators needed the additional market strength so they could unload their holdings without toppling the market too soon. And at market bottoms, they manipulated the thinking of public investors to keep them out of the market and selling while the manipulators loaded up again at the low prices.

Has that changed?

Did something change in modern times that caused experienced investors and Wall Street institutions to now believe, as they advise public investors, that the stock market cannot be 'timed', that buy and hold investing is the way to investing success?

Let's look at the investment strategies of today's professional investors, which include mutual funds, brokerage firms, investment banks, corporate insiders, and today's wealthy private investors, *when they are investing their own money.*

MUTUAL FUNDS:

It's understandable that mutual funds would not want their investors to realize that buy and hold investing does not work. Their own profit depends on the management fees they receive for operating the fund, and those fees are based on a percentage of the assets in the fund. How would they survive if every once in awhile, as a serious correction or bear market approaches, large numbers of investors took their money away, perhaps moving it to foreign markets, gold, cash, bonds, real estate, or whatever?

Not only would the revenues of the mutual funds plunge, but if they let their investors get away, could they be sure when they came back to the market that they would come back to the same funds? Or would they choose a competitor's fund for some reason, perhaps because it had better performance the previous year?

- So it's easy enough to understand that mutual fund managers must do all they can to convince investors that market-timing does not work.

But do they actually believe it?

We don't have to guess or surmise. The evidence is quite clear in the published portfolio turnover rates of mutual funds.

Forty to fifty years ago, when the concept of mutual funds was just beginning in earnest, most early funds did indeed buy and hold the stocks in their portfolios. Statistics show that the average portfolio holding period for funds in the 1960s was about six years.

However, in 1977 a revolutionary change took place in mutual fund management. Peter Lynch became manager of the then tiny Fidelity Magellan Fund. With an aggressive style that for years included an average annual portfolio turnover rate of around 300%, he soon had the Magellan Fund significantly outperforming the market, and its peers.

As a result Lynch was on his way to being considered the best mutual fund manager of the times. Yes, a 300% average portfolio turnover rate means an average holding period of just 4 months for all the stocks in the portfolio. Since there must have been some core holdings that were held for longer periods, we can conclude that Lynch was holding many stocks for even less than four months. And he was beating the pants off his competitors.

Since as we discussed earlier, money chases performance, Fidelity's Magellan Fund was soon on its way to becoming the largest mutual fund in history. Other fund-managers took notice. Some began following a similar strategy of taking profits more quickly and moving on, also producing superior results that caused investors to pile into their funds. The mutual fund industry was learning the importance of market-timing as opposed to buy and hold investing.

The following table shows how portfolio turnover rates for some of the funds that became the largest and most popular had changed by the mid-1990s.

	ANNUAL PORTFOLIO TURNOVER RATE				
FUND	1993	1994	1995	1996	1997
AIM WEINGARTEN A	109%	136%	139%	159%	-
AARP CAPITAL GROWTH	101%	80%	98%	65%	39%
BERGER 100 FUND	74%	64%	114%	122%	200%
CGM CAPITAL DEVELOPMENT	143%	146%	271%	178%	-
DREYFUS FUND	39%	28%	269%	221%	201%
FIDELITY MAGELLAN	155%	132%	120%	155%	67%
INVESCO DYNAMIC	144%	169%	175%	196%	204%
JANUS FUND	127%	139%	118%	104%	132%
KEMPER TOTAL RETURN	180%	121%	142%	85%	122%
PHOENIX BALANCED	130%	159%	197%	191%	206%
SMITH BARNEY MNGD MUNIS	206%	131%	100%	80%	103%
STRONG TOTAL RETURN	271%	290%	un-known	502%	un-known
TEMPLETON GLOBAL INCOME	265%	138%	104%	113%	192%
Average:	149%	133%	154%	167%	147%

Note the portfolio turnover rate of the Templeton Global Income Fund. John Templeton is most famous for publicly insisting that buying and holding for the long-term is the only way to investing success. It's also interesting that after Fidelity Magellan Fund manager Peter Lynch was promoted to Vice-President at Fidelity, he wrote numerous best-selling books calling for investors to simply choose good stocks and hold them forever.

In any event, despite the propaganda from mutual fund executives that buy and hold is the way to investing success, by 1999 Morningstar Inc. reported that the average portfolio turnover rates of *all* the mutual funds within the universe of those it tracks, was as follows, broken down by their investment strategies.

	Growth Funds	Value Funds	Average
Portfolio turnover	122%	69%	96%

Keep in mind that the above tables show mutual fund portfolio turnover rates in the longest and most one-sided bull market in history. If ever there were a time when mutual funds could be expected to buy and hold, if that is the strategy that works, and the strategy they really believe in, the decade of the 1990s was it. Yet mutual funds kept holdings for a matter of months, not years.

Since the year 2000 the annual portfolio turnover rates of mutual funds has increased even more, averaging 111%.

YET—MUTUAL FUNDS HAVE MARKET-TIMING LIMITATIONS.

While certainly not engaged in buy and hold investing, mutual funds are limited in how far they can go in timing the market. They can 'time' individual stocks, holding them for short periods, taking profits and moving on to different holdings. And they certainly do that.

However, they cannot time the overall market by for instance moving to cash in times of high risk. They must remain very close to fully invested at all times.

As a result, when the overall market declines substantially, as in a bear market, and carries most everything down with it, mutual funds have no way to escape the losses.

Why do the prospectuses of most mutual funds require the fund to remain just about fully invested all the time, even though at times its manager believes the overall market is in for a significant decline?

Because investors, and particularly money-management firms, need to know if they want to be 60% in stocks and 40% in bonds, that when they send 60% of their assets to an equity mutual fund the fund will remain 100% invested in the market. If the mutual fund manager decided market risk was too high, and moved the fund to only 50% invested, those investors would unknowingly be only 30% in stocks, with an unintended 30% in cash. Therefore, even in serious market declines mutual funds remain fully invested.

- It is up to investors in those funds to know enough to cut back exposure to the market when risk is high of a correction. The mutual fund manager will not do that for them!

The limitations on how aggressively mutual funds can engage in market-timing led to the introduction and popularity of hedge funds.

SO THEN, ARE HEDGE-FUNDS BUY & HOLD INVESTORS?

In the early 1990s there were perhaps a hundred or so 'hedge-funds' in existence. In recent years, the growth of such funds as the investment choice of wealthy and sophisticated investors has been explosive. In 2007 there are more than 8,000 such funds, with a total of more than $1.4 trillion under management.

What is a hedge-fund?

A hedge-fund is actually a private investment limited liability partnership, or LLP. The manager of the fund is the general partner, making all the decisions and running the fund. The investors are limited partners in the LLP. As long as the fund, its general partner, and the limited partners meet certain requirements, hedge funds can avoid most of the regulations and restrictions under which U.S. mutual funds and money-managers operate.

Those requirements include that the LLP must limit itself to no more than 99 investors (limited partners). In addition, each of those investors must be a 'qualified' investor. That means they must certify that they understand and can afford the risk of aggressive investing, have a minimum net worth of a million dollars, and a six figure income. A hedge-fund cannot advertise, and cannot even approach a potential investor regarding the fund without knowing in advance that the potential investor meets all the requirements for certification as a qualified investor.

Because hedge-funds are limited to so few investors they generally require very high minimum investments by their limited partners, one to five million dollars being common. The high minimums also lessen the chance they might inadvertently take in an unqualified investor. That is important since should they do so they run the risk of losing their exemption from regulations.

However, if all the restrictions and qualifications are met, the hedge-fund (LLP) can operate mostly unfettered by U.S. regulations that are in place to protect unsophisticated investors, and under which conventional money-managers, financial planners, and mutual funds must operate.

Hedge-funds are therefore free to invest in any area where they see a profit opportunity; stocks, bonds, currencies, commodities, real estate, foreign markets, etc. More importantly, they can leverage their positions dramatically through the use of margin, loans, options, futures, and complex derivative strategies. In expectation of market declines, they are not only free to move to 100% cash, but can go after profits from the downside through the use of short-sales and leveraged downside positioning.

The attraction of hedge funds to those who launch them is that, unlike conventional money-managers, hedge fund managers are allowed to share in the profits they make for their investors.

The typical arrangement for a normal money-management firm is to charge each client an annual fee of 1% to 2% of the amount of money they have under management for that client. However, the typical arrangement for a hedge fund is for the general partner (hedge-fund manager) to receive an annual management fee of 2% of the money under management, *plus* 20% of the annual profits. In the industry it's known as 'two and twenty fees'.

In the early 1980s there were only a few hedge-funds, most notably those of George Soros, Michael Steinhardt, and Julian Robertson. They became hugely famous by making fortunes for their investors, as well as for themselves, through aggressive market-timing in global stock, currency, and commodity markets.

The power of their leveraged positions was such that foreign central banks sometimes blamed the ups and downs of their currencies on one or the other of the large hedge funds. For instance, hedge funds were implicated in the 1992 crisis that led to major exchange rate realignments in the European Monetary System. They were suspected of creating the period of wild turbulence in international bond markets in 1994, and the financial upheavals in Asia in 1997.

The publicity regarding their aggressiveness, and huge profits, created great interest in hedge-funds, and as mentioned, the number of such funds has grown from only a hundred or so in the 1980s to more than 8,000 by 2007.

Due to their secrecy it is difficult to pin down their performance. However, the fact that sophisticated investors have poured more than $1.4 trillion into them in recent years, at the cost of having to pay the managers 20% of any profits, is a fair indication of significant satisfaction with their performance.

Obviously, not one of those 8,000 hedge-funds is operated on anything near a buy & hold strategy. On the contrary, their appeal and strategy is that they are deliberately set up so they can engage in market-timing to a dramatic degree.

So, if mutual funds and hedge funds rely on significant market-timing for their success, where might we find Wall Street institutions and professionals who actually believe what they tell the public, that buy & hold is the way to go, that the market cannot be timed?

How about:

CORPORATE INSIDERS:

Periodic scandals and investigations after every market plunge of the last 200 years, including after the recent 2000-2002 bear market, showed how insiders of the *illegal* variety are very successful with market-timing. They tip off relatives and friends to upcoming deals before they become public knowledge, or bail out of their bankrupt stock at very high prices before it implodes. Some of those who are caught wind up doing time.

However, I'm not talking about illegal insider trading. I'm talking about legal management of their private investments by those who happen to have careers in corporate management, or are on the board of directors of publicly held companies.

Such corporate insiders are allowed to trade in and out of their stocks with few restrictions, as long as they don't make trades based on information before it becomes available to the public. They must also report the changes in their holdings to the Securities and Exchange Commission (SEC) in a timely manner.

It's clear why corporate insiders would not want investors trading in and out of their stocks, adding to the normal up and down volatility in the price of the stock.

It's particularly understandable why they do not want investors bailing out to any degree in advance of economic downturns or bear markets. That might be just the time when corporations need their stock prices to hold up as well as possible, for use as collateral for loans, or in acquisitions of competitors. It might also be just the time when corporate insiders want to sell some of their own holdings, and don't want public investors also selling and driving the price down on them.

However, it's just as clear that corporate insiders do not follow a buy and hold strategy with their own money. They cannot hide their activities. As mentioned, SEC rules require that insiders file all changes in their stock holdings, usually within three days.

There are often attempts to delay those filings, or to disguise them. But month after month, year after year, those filings clearly show how persistently and successfully company insiders trade in and out of their company's stock, selling after prices have rallied, but before they begin to decline, and buying back after the stock has declined to lower levels.

They should not be criticized for that. It is their own usually hard-earned money, and they are only engaging in the most important rule of successful investing, buying low and selling high.

There are no statistics available as to whether their market-timing produces better performance for them than buy and hold. However, they know more about their company's prospects at any time, whether sales are rising or slowing, whether a new product has prospects or problems, whether costs are rising or coming under control, than could any outsider. So it should be no surprise that anecdotal evidence indicates they have considerable success with their market-timing activities.

In fact, that evidence is so strong that Wall Street professionals and astute investors use measurements of which companies have insiders buying, and which have insiders selling, as important research to guide their own investments. There are even research firms set up solely to record and analyze the activity of corporate insiders, selling that information to investors, money-managers, and Wall Street institutions.

LUCKY INSIDERS

All too often when a company reveals some piece of negative news that causes its stock to plunge, it is later revealed in SEC filings that the company's insiders had already sold their stock prior to releasing the negative news. Too many times it also turns out they were making the rounds of the financial circuit touting the stock to the public as a great buy even as they were selling their own shares.

Asked about it, they invariably reply that they had no advance knowledge of the bad news. They sold their stock "only to diversify my investments", or "for personal reasons", and by coincidence the company ran into a problem almost immediately.

Insiders seem to also have a lucky knack in timing their purchases. In a study conducted by Measured Markets Inc. for The New York Times, the researchers found that 41% of all stocks related to mergers and acquisitions showed suspicious insider trading activity before the buyout bids were made public.

It appears that corporate insiders not only engage in market-timing, but in doing so may sometimes take advantage of public investors for their market-timing profits, selling their stock while telling investors it's time to buy, or buying in advance of the public learning of a pending merger or acquisition deal. Just another example of how the Wall Street playing field, where investors choose to play against the pros, is tilted in the favor of the pros.

So where does that leave us in our search for successful investors who believe the market cannot be timed?

If mutual funds turn their portfolios over in a matter of months not years; if 8,000 hedge-fund managers engage in even more dramatic market-timing than regular mutual funds; if corporate insiders trade in and out of their stocks depending on market conditions; how about:

BROKERAGE FIRMS.

Brokerage firms primarily trade for their own accounts via a process known as 'program-trading'.

Using massive computers and sophisticated computer programs they are able to react instantly with computerized 'buy programs' when a piece of market-moving news crosses the newswires. That puts those firms instantly in the market when news breaks, before other investors can react. They usually hold those positions for only a few hours. As soon as there are signs that the news has brought in all the public buying or selling that can be expected, resulting in a short-term pop-up in the stock price, the program-trading firms close out their positions (via instant computerized 'sell programs'), and wait for the next piece of quick news.

Another form of their program-trading is known as arbitrage. Their complex computer programs continuously track various markets. When they spot a discrepancy between markets, a so-called 'anomaly', they pounce with their large buy and sell programs.

For instance, if their computers spot that the S&P 500 index on the 'cash' stock market (the normal trading of shares on the New York Stock Exchange), is out of synch with the value of the S&P 500 in the futures market at the Chicago Board of Trade, by a few pennies, the computers will pounce. They enter a huge buy program on one market and a simultaneous sell program on the other market, profiting from that small difference in pricing between the two markets. They pick up only a few pennies per share in profit. But they trade so many millions of dollars of stock with each trade that the profit becomes worth the effort, especially since the process is often repeated several times a day. Holding times? Usually only a few minutes. As soon as the two markets are back in synch, producing the small profits, the computers execute reverse trades that close out the positions.

- As unbelievable as it seems, program-trading accounts for more than half of the total daily trading volume on the NYSE. Think about that. More than half of all the trades in the stock market are the huge buy and sell programs of program-trading firms, in which the holding periods average less than a full day.

Who are these large program-trading firms?

Those accounting for most of the program trading each week are listed in financial publications like *Barron's*. The list is always of some of the largest brokerage firms and investment banks; Bear Stearns, Goldman Sachs, Merrill Lynch, Bank of America, Citigroup, Deutsche Banc, Lehman Brothers, RBC Capital Markets (Royal Bank of Canada), Credit Suisse First Boston, Morgan Stanley, UBS Securities, and others.

Their retail branches, and their media spokesmen, may tell public investors to simply buy and hold because the market cannot be timed. But isn't it interesting that brokerage firms and investment banks trading for their own accounts rarely risk their own money by holding even overnight.

So *now* where are we in our search for successful investors who believe the market cannot be timed? Mutual funds turn their portfolios over in a matter of months not years; 8,000 hedge-fund managers engage in even more dramatic market-timing; corporate insiders trade in and out of their stocks depending on market conditions; brokerage firms jump in and out with buy and sell programs the frequency of which can only be described as frenetic. Then how about:

BIG-NAME INVESTORS.

Surely if Wall Street is correct that the market cannot be timed, we should find that the vast majority of well-known successful private investors avoid market-timing.

But yet, as I mentioned before, those that emerged from a previous era with huge fortunes, Joseph P. Kennedy, Bernard Baruch, Jesse Livermore, J.P. Morgan, E.H. Harriman, William Danforth, Jay Gould, Jim Fisk, Cornelius Vanderbilt, and many others, were all aggressive market-timers. Not a buy and hold investor in the lot.

That remains true in the current generation of famous investors. The likes of George Soros, Paul Tudor Jones, Julian Robertson, Richard Rainwater, Michael Steinhardt, mutual fund managers like Bill Gross, Peter Lynch, Michael Price, Jeffrey Vinik. All are market-timers.

The next time someone tells you the best way to invest is to buy and hold, that the market can't be timed, (because that's what they've heard so often from Wall Street), challenge him or her to name *anyone* who has become an outstanding investor by adopting such a strategy.

The first and probably only name they can come up with will be that of Warren Buffett.

Just tell them they are very, very wrong.

And if even Warren Buffett, reputed to be the most successful investor of all time, is a market-timer, that should put an end to the argument.

Chapter 5

Warren Buffett, Market-Timer Extraordinaire

Warren Buffett carefully nurtures his image as a simple, small-town, aw-shucks investor in Omaha, Nebraska (whose strategy anyone can emulate). He is famous for such quotes as, *"I simply pick stocks based on whether a company is one I'd like to own even if there were no stock market"*, and *"My favorite holding time is forever."*

No wonder then that investors have the impression that Buffett is a buy and hold investor, who by simply buying 'good stocks' and holding them forever, became a multi-billionaire. No wonder they think that if they can find out what stocks he is buying it would be safe to also buy them, since he will be holding them 'forever'.

Let's look into why they are so often disappointed by their results.

Why would Buffett want public investors to believe he is a buy and hold investor and they should follow his example?

He has the same motivation as a mutual fund manager in that regard.

Buffett's huge holding company, Berkshire Hathaway, is a publicly traded company, trading on the NYSE. It's similar to a mutual fund in that it's a holding company of the investments that Buffett makes, whether in companies that Berkshire Hathaway acquires as wholly-owned subsidiaries, or investments it makes in publicly traded companies.

Were its stock-holders to engage in market-timing, selling their Berkshire Hathaway stock at its highs and buying back at its lows, it would cause numerous problems for Buffett. For instance, their periodic selling would add significantly to the already high volatility of Berkshire's stock price.

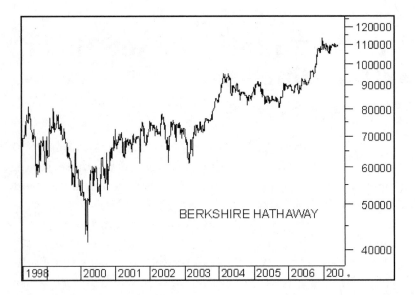

Yes, even though the common perception is that investing with Buffett must be stress-free for his fortunate investors, the stocks that Buffett invests in, and therefore Berkshire Hathaway stock, suffer the same periodic ups and downs as the rest of the stock market.

As the above chart shows, it plunged 32% in 1998, 49% in 1999, 23% in 2002, and 18% in 2004-2005. Anyone buying at its peak in 1999 waited five years, until 2004, to get back to even.

But I digress. Is Buffett really a buy and hold investor that any public investor can emulate? Or is he one of the well-trained and equipped professionals who live and breathe the market, playing hardball with the other professionals on Wall Street's game field?

- To begin with, Buffett is anything but the unsophisticated 'aw shucks' country bumpkin investor of folklore.

In fact, there are few participants in the securities industry that could come close to matching his training, education, contacts, and experience in economics, business, and markets.

Buffett's father owned a brokerage firm in Omaha, Nebraska. At a very young age, Buffett was being steeped in the intricacies of the economy, stock market, and investing. At the age of eleven he was already working at his father's firm after school and during summer vacations. Upon college graduation, Buffet entered graduate school at Columbia University in New York, where he studied under famed professor and market statistician Benjamin Graham. Graham took a liking to Buffett and became his mentor. After graduating from Columbia with a Masters degree in economics, Buffett returned to Omaha to gain experience at his father's brokerage and investment banking company for awhile. He then returned to New York City, where he spent two years as an analyst at Benjamin Graham's highly regarded market research firm.

In 1956, back in Omaha, armed with more economic and market education, mentoring, and experience at the age of 27 than most professionals gain in a lifetime, he launched Buffett Partnership, Ltd. It was a limited partnership investment company similar in make-up to the hedge-funds of today. Its investors were primarily clients of his father's firm. They became limited partners. Buffett was the general partner, in charge of the operation.

He managed that private fund with considerable success from 1957 to 1969, significantly beating the market, with performance that would have turned an investor's $10,000 into $300,000 over the period.

Given the secrecy of private investment companies, it's impossible to know to what degree he engaged in portfolio-turnover and market-timing. But common sense says that one does not turn $10,000 into $300,000 in 12 years by simply buying and holding stocks in a market that averages gains of 12.5% a year. It would require leverage and considerable in and out trading, taking profits on winners when they became overbought, and moving on to stocks that had not yet made significant gains.

But we do know positively that he pulled off one of the most dramatic market-timing moves of all time.

At age 39, after making huge gains in the mid-1960s bull market, he cashed out *entirely* in early 1969. While the exciting bull market of the 1960s had investors still piling into the stock market in 1969, Buffett completely walked away from it. He liquidated his investment partnership and dispersed the assets to his investors. He told his investors they would probably be better off in government bonds for awhile. His generous general partner's share made Buffett a very wealthy man at a young age.

Buffett stayed completely away from the stock market for several years. He settled back to manage the businesses he had acquired control of on the side, including Diversified Retailing Inc. (a chain of women's apparel stores), and Berkshire Hathaway, a textile mill in New Bedford, Mass. He sold Berkshire's mill operations and began turning Berkshire Hathaway into a conglomerate of wholly-owned companies through acquisitions. The early acquisitions included See's Candies, The Omaha Sun, and most importantly, Geico Insurance. The businesses did well under Buffett's management.

With exquisite market-timing, having exited the market completely near the 1969 bull market top, he stayed away until 1974.

Then, after yet another bear market, the serious bear of 1973-74 in which the Dow lost 45% of its value, Buffett provided another impressive example of market-timing.

Believing that prices had reached a long-term low, he returned to the market.

In a famous 1974 interview in Forbe's magazine he said, "This is the time to start investing again."

And he did, using his control of publicly traded Berkshire Hathaway as the holding company for his investments.

It's important that investors realize that his re-entry into the stock market meant he was again investing in publicly traded stocks, but Buffett also continued to have Berkshire Hathaway acquire businesses that it would manage and operate as subsidiaries.

As a result, over the years Berkshire Hathaway has grown into a huge conglomerate of more than forty wholly-owned subsidiaries. They include Geico Insurance, Acme Bricks, Benjamin Moore Paints, Clayton Homes, Nebraska Furniture Mart, Borshein's Jew-

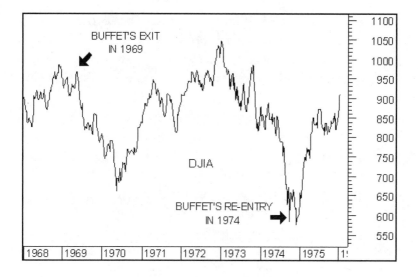

elry, See's Candies, World Book Encyclopedias, Fruit of the Loom, General Re Insurance, Johns Manville, Dairy Queen, Shaw Industries, NetJets, Flight Safety International, and twenty-five others. That these businesses were acquired in total, to become wholly-owned operating subsidiaries of Berkshire Hathaway, gave rise to the myth that Buffett buys and holds all investments for the very long-term.

However, when it comes to Buffett's (Berkshire Hathaway's) investments in the stock market, very few stocks have been long-term holdings.

Even during the long one-sided 1990s bull market, which favored buy and hold investing, SEC filings show that Buffett traded in and out of huge holdings in Salomon Bros., U.S. Air Group, McDonald's, Target, Sealed Air, Outback Steakhouse, Pier 1 Imports, Comcast, Disney, Freddie Mac, zero coupon bonds, silver, the U.S. dollar, foreign bonds, currencies, and many more.

Buffett, or Berkshire Hathaway, will occasionally reveal that the company has taken a significant position in a stock, and public investors, believing that Buffett buys and hold stocks 'forever' will scramble into it, often driving the price higher. Fairly often when Berkshire Hathaway makes its annual report of holdings, investors will discover Berkshire Hathaway no longer holds the stock, *may* have been selling it even as investors were buying it.

Buy & hold investing of businesses it will own entirely and run as a wholly owned subsidiary 'forever'? Absolutely. Buy & hold investing in publicly traded stocks? Not hardly.

Examples of Buffett's investment decisions involving market-timing are too many to cover in detail. But for instance, when Buffett thought market risk was getting too high in 1999, he raised Berkshire Hathaway's cash levels to a huge $50 billion. He didn't refer to even that as market-timing, but said, "I just can't find anything I want to invest in right now." But to have raised $50 billion in cash must have required some serious unloading of stocks. And it was good timing, since the serious 2000-2002 bear market was soon underway.

In 2005, after participating in the new bull market that began in 2002, Buffett again moved $40 billion into cash, shying away from the U.S. stock market and U.S. bonds.

If one pays attention to what he says, he does advocate market-timing even publicly, making no bones about advice to get out early when risk becomes high. Some of his quotes in that regard include:

- *"At the start of the party the punch is flowing and everything's going well, but you know at midnight it's all going to turn into pumpkins and mice. People think they'll be able to get out just before midnight, but everyone else thinks that too."*

- *"What the wise man does at the beginning [of a rising market] the fool does at the end. Once a price history [rising market] develops enough for other people to see it and get envious, greed takes over markets."*

- *"We simply attempt to be fearful when others are greedy, and greedy when others are fearful."*

An unsophisticated buy & hold country-boy investor who believes that markets cannot be timed? Not hardly. Buffett is a highly educated economist and portfolio-manager, nurtured in investing from an early age, wealthy at a young age from operating a private-investment limited partnership of wealthy clients of his father's investment bank.

He has been on the boards of numerous corporations and banks from an early age, obtaining important insider information, and has a clear history of major market-timing of the overall market, as well as timing of individual stocks, silver, bonds, and international currencies.

Analysts also seem to miss the fact that more than half of Berkshire Hathaway's annual profits come not from profits on its investments in publicly traded companies, but from the operating earnings of its more than forty subsidiaries; Clayton Homes, Dairy Queen, Geico, Net Jets, et al.

So then; who is left who might think of themselves as buy and hold investors, those who believe the market cannot be timed?

Yes, we have finally found them, and they are:

PUBLIC INVESTORS.

- Those public investors who believe Wall Street's hype. Those widows and orphans who held onto AT&T and General Motors, or U.S. Steel and Westinghouse, because daddy left it to them, saying, "Don't ever sell the AT&T", (or GM or whatever).

- Those public investors who sold out at the bottom of bear markets or serious market corrections with large losses, only to see 'the market', but probably not their specific portfolios, eventually 'come back'. They believe that market-timing doesn't work, not only because Wall Street tells them so, but because their version of market-timing, buying near the tops and selling in disgust after major declines have devastated their portfolios, didn't work.

Chapter 6

Market Risk—Sector Risk—Stock Risk

Okay, so you realize that buy and hold doesn't work. You also realize that mutual funds, money-managers and other professionals, know that, and so depend on market-timing.

Yet 80% of mutual funds, money managers, and professionals fail to match the performance of the benchmark S&P 500 over the long-term.

So what are you to do to be successful in your investing? Buy and hold is a sham and cannot work. Yet even highly trained and equipped professionals have problems trying to even match the performance of the market over the long-term through market-timing.

Many non-professional investors believe that with a little luck they can simply do a better job of it than the professionals.

To see how probable that might be, let's begin by looking briefly at the three risks of investing in the stock market.

MARKET RISK:

The most obvious investing risk is that the overall market may not move in the direction you expect.

When the market goes up it carries the majority of stocks, sectors, and mutual funds up with it, as in the old market maxim, 'A rising tide lifts all boats'.

- That ability of the market to pull even bad stocks, sectors, and mutual funds up with it is also reflected in the old maxim that,

"There is nothing like a bull market to convince an investor that he or she is an investing genius."

However, when the market goes down, unfortunately it carries most stocks, sectors, and mutual funds, *even good ones*, down with it. So even if you have chosen a stock well, the odds are that it will be pulled down if the overall market declines.

- That led to an equally true maxim that, "There is nothing like a bear market to disabuse an investor of the notion that he is an investing genius".

SECTOR RISK.

The second risk in the stock market is sector risk.

Even though the overall market may go up, there are always sectors that do not move as much as the market, and will therefore not match the market's performance. Some sectors may even move opposite to the direction of the overall market.

For instance, in the rip-roaring final year of the 1990s bull market, while the tech, biotech, and telecom sectors blew the roof off, sectors like autos, energy, food, gold, insurance, and paper products, suffered serious declines.

More recently, in 2006, the overall market enjoyed above average performance, the S&P 500 gaining 15.4% (including dividends). However, there were many opportunities to be in the wrong sectors, or to even be down for the year. Much of the overall market's gain in 2006 was the result of strength in the financial, energy, and commodity sectors. Sectors including healthcare, information technology, consumer discretionary, and homebuilding, lagged far behind.

STOCK RISK.

The third risk is individual company, or stock risk. Even when an investor is right on overall market direction, *and* on sector selection, he (or she) still may choose stocks that will have problems of their own.

For instance, again in the final bubble years of the 1990s bull market, the overall stock market, and the semi-conductor sector, and most stocks within that sector soared. However, investors in popular semiconductor maker Advanced Micro Circuits saw its stock plunge 65%.

More recently, Cisco Systems, and Hewlett Packard, in the technology sector, gained 59% and 45% respectively in 2006. However, Dell Computer and Xilinx lost 16%, and 30% respectively. In the biotechnology sector, Biogen was up 10% for 2006, while Amgen was down 15%.

AVOIDING MUCH OF THE RISK.

Obviously then, in making an individual stock-picking selection, an investor needs to be right that the overall market is likely to go up, since if it instead goes down, the investor is liable to see his good stock go down due to market forces, rather than see it go up due to its own merits.

In his stock-picking analysis an investor needs to also be right that even if the overall market moves higher, the sector the stock is in will also move higher by at least the same degree.

Finally, the investor needs to be right that even if the market *and* the stock's sector go up, this particular company's stock will also go up.

Too often investors get excited about a stock tip, or a stock's previous performance, and expect it will go up regardless of what the market or its sector does. Not impossible, but it would be a rare stock.

Studies show that market, sector, and stock risk are approximately equal. Therefore, there are simple ways to decrease investing risk significantly.

Sector Investing.

Obviously an investor could eliminate one third of investing risk by simply investing in market sectors rather than in individual stocks.

Today's investors are able to accomplish that with ease.

Sector Mutual Funds.

Numerous mutual fund families, Fidelity, Vanguard, Rydex, Pro-Funds, and others, have offered mutual funds designed to track with specific sectors for years. Some also offer 'inverse' funds, which move opposite to the underlying sector, which investors can use to make profits in a declining market.

However, in recent years many mutual fund families have made it more difficult, or at least more expensive, for individual investors to invest in their sector funds.

Rather than administer hundreds of thousands of individual accounts and the paper work that entails, they prefer that individual investors use the services of a money management firm. Money management firms make a single large 'block' trade for all their clients at once, much easier for the mutual funds to handle.

Another problem mutual funds have with individual investors is that individual investors engage in far more in and out short-term trading than do money management firms.

So in recent years many mutual funds have imposed minimum holding periods of three to six months on individual investors, and charge 'early withdrawal' fees of as much as 2% on those who need to exit sooner.

Therefore, investors considering such funds for market-timing purposes need to perform a certain amount of due diligence in making their choices. For instance, at the present time anyway, Rydex and ProFunds do not impose minimum holding periods or early withdrawal fees on most of their funds, while Fidelity and Vanguard do.

Exchange-Traded-Funds.

The unfriendliness toward individual investors which has taken place in many regular mutual fund families that had previously catered to individual investors, created an opportunity for a different product from Wall Street.

Exchange-traded-funds (ETFs) were introduced. ETFs trade on major stock exchanges, and can be bought and sold like a stock, through any brokerage firm, with no minimum holding periods. Their appeal was instant, and their popularity has grown dramatically.

By early 2007 there were already 690 ETFs in existence, offering diversified portfolios focused on the overall market (index funds) as well as specific sectors of the market, and more being created weekly.

A few examples of ETFs designed to track with a specific sector;

Sector ETF	Ticker Symbol
Biotechnology SPDR	XLB
iShares Biotechnology	BBH
Computer Software HOLDR	SWH
Consumer Staples SPDR	XLP
Consumer Discretionary	XLY
Energy SPDR	XLE
Rydex S&P Energy	RYE
Financial SPDR	XLF
Rydex S&P Financials	RYF
streetTracks Gold Trust	GLD
iShares Healthcare	IYH
Internet HOLDR	HHH
Industrial SPDR	XLI
Oil Services HOLDR	OIH
Pharmaceutical HOLDR	PPH
iShares Real Estate Trusts	IYR
Retail HOLDR	RTH
Semiconductor HOLDR	SMH
Technology SPDR	XLK
Rydex S&P Technology	RYT
iShares Telecommunications	IYZ
Utilities SPDR	XLU

In late 2006, and early 2007, ProFunds Inc. introduced its ProShares leveraged 'double-inverse' ETFs. Like all ETFs, they trade like a stock, are purchased through brokerage firms, and have no minimum holding period.

They allow investors to bet on a *decline* in individual sectors. They're designed not only to move opposite to the underlying sector, but are leveraged to move *twice as much* as the sector. That is, if the sector moves down 10%, the leveraged 'inverse' ETF is designed to move up 20%.

Investors need to understand that leverage is a two-edged sword. It doubles the profits when one is right, but also doubles the loss when one is wrong. Following are examples of leveraged 'double-inverse' ETFs:

Inverse Sector ETFs	Symbol
ProShares Ultra-Short Basic Materials Sector	SMN
ProShares Ultra-Short Consumer Goods Sector	SZK
ProShares Ultra-Short Financial Sector	SKF
ProShares Ultra-Short Healthcare Sector	RXD
ProShares Ultra-Short Industrials Sector	SIJ
ProShares Ultra-Short Real Estate Sector	SRS
ProShares Ultra-Short Technology Sector	REW
ProShares Ultra-Short Utilities Sector	SDP

Yes, the tools and products investors have available to take advantage of any kind of market condition have changed dramatically just within the last few years.

However, while sector investing eliminates individual stock risk, it still involves both sector and market risk.

An investor can take another step, and eliminate both stock *and* sector risk, by investing only in the overall market.

Since theoretically stock risk, sector risk, and market risk are

approximately equal, an investor doing so eliminates two-thirds of the risk of investing in the stock market.

INVESTING ONLY IN THE OVERALL MARKET.

Now we're getting closer to the strategy I promised, which has doubled and tripled the performance of the S&P 500 over the last 50 years. It begins with an understanding of 'index' funds.

The first index mutual fund, the Vanguard S&P 500 Index Fund, was designed to track with the performance of the S&P 500. It was introduced in 1976.

The concept was ridiculed at the time, described as 'Bogle's Folly', in a swipe at Vanguard chairman John Bogle. After all, at best the fund could only *match* the performance of the S&P 500. By its very design it guaranteed that on a buy & hold basis it could not possibly outperform the index.

So the critics asked why investors should settle for that when they could perhaps latch onto the next Microsoft or WalMart, or get into the tech sector, or emerging markets, in time for their next huge move up?

Bogle argued that most investors, including professionals, were unable to beat, or even match, the performance of the S&P 500 over the long-term. Better performance could therefore be guaranteed for most by simply investing directly in the index.

However in 1976 when the index fund was introduced, the 1973-74 bear market had ended and the next bull market was underway. So investors were confident and optimistic, convinced that by picking well-managed mutual funds, or through their own superior stock-picking, they could easily out-perform the S&P 500. The Vanguard S&P 500 Index fund was of no interest.

Unfortunately for investors, by early 1977 the next bear market had begun, and the market suffered *two more* over the next seven years.

As usual, managed mutual funds, money-managers, and particularly individual investors, did not handle them well.

The tendency, as it has always been, was to be optimistic and

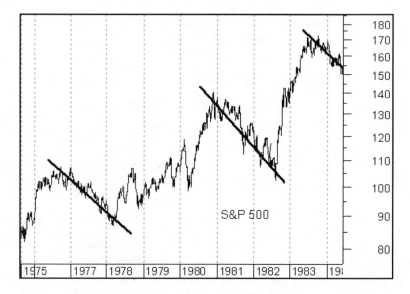

confident by the time the market reached tops, and to become even more fully invested as the market declined, by 'buying the dips'. Once again, only after serious portfolio damage was done did most investors bail out in disgust near the lows. And then they did not re-enter in time to make the gains when the index recovered.

Bogle and his Vanguard Funds advertised throughout the period that investors in their S&P 500 Index Fund *were* matching the performance of the index.

Thus did index investing become popular. Investors, suffering losses time after time by trying to beat the market, finally decided they would be happy after all if they could just be assured of matching the market's performance.

The Vanguard S&P 500 Index fund soon became the largest mutual fund in the world. Other mutual fund families began offering similar index funds, until today an S&P 500 index fund is available at virtually all multiple-fund families.

However, their popularity waned again in the mid-1990s, when once again a bull market convinced investors that investing was easy and they could beat the performance even of a soaring bull market.

Beginning in 1995, a relatively few sectors and individual stocks, notably in the internet and high-tech sectors, began exploding upward, outperforming the market indexes, and creating a lot of excitement.

Investors scrambled out of index funds and into those hottest sectors, and into the exciting individual stocks within those hot sectors.

For several years it paid off big-time, as the unusual 1990s bull market set a record for longevity. For instance, even as the S&P 500 index rose 28% in 1998, and 20.1% in 1999, providing superior returns, the technology sector rose 78% in 1998, and 77% in 1999.

However, the cycle of bull and bear markets had not gone away, although many believed that to be the case at the time. The wildly popular high-tech stocks in particular soared like Roman candles, and then also like Roman candles sputtered and plunged back to the ground in the severe 2000-2002 bear market that followed. Investors were again disabused of the notion that they could outperform the market through superior stock or sector selection.

The technology sector gave up all of its big gains of 1998 and 1999.

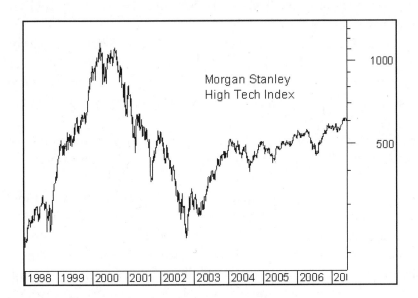

Even so, index fund investing still has not returned to its previous popularity. With the arrival of the new bull market in 2002, investors picked up the pieces of what was left of their portfolios and began to dream again of being able to beat the market through superior stock or sector selection.

So what don't they like about index funds?

Many investors dislike index funds on the grounds that not all the stocks in an index will go up even if the index itself goes up. And that is true. So why not pick the individual stocks within the index that are likely to go up the most, and avoid those that are likely to go down?

Well, that is not a startling new approach. It is exactly what every investor, professional and non-professional, is *trying* to accomplish. And we have seen the statistics of how poorly they do, unable to even *match* the performance of the indexes, let alone beat them.

For instance, let's look at the performance over the last cycle of the Dow and the 30 stocks that make up that index. Since the Dow has led the way back in recovering from the 2000-2002 bear market, it should have been the easiest source of winning stocks in recent years.

The Dow lost 38.7% of its value in the 2000-2002 bear market. By late 2006, the Dow had climbed back up to its previous peak of January 14, 2000. By May 2007, as this is being written, the Dow has rallied further and is at a new record high, 15.5% *above* its peak of January, 2000.

However, 16 of the 30 stocks in the index, *more than half*, are actually still below their levels at the Dow's peak on January 14, 2000, and not by a small amount but by *an average of 30%*.

How could the Dow be making new record highs with more than half of the stocks in the index still down an average of 30%? Because the recovery of the Dow has been substantially due to unusual gains by just 6 stocks. Those six stocks, Minnesota Mining & Manufacturing, Altria (formerly Phillip Morris), Boeing, Caterpillar, Exxon-Mobil, and United Technologies, have rallied so strongly since 2000 that they are more than 100% above their price at the Dow's peak in 2000.

	Price Jan. 14, 2000	Price mid-May, 2007	Difference
DJIA INDEX	11,723	13,539	+ 15.5%
DJIA Components			
Alcoa	40.00	45.36	+ 13.4%
Altria	24.25	71.68	+ 195.6%
AIG Group	76.04	71.94	**- 5.4%**
American Express	53.16	64.27	+ 20.9%
A T & T	137.00	40.44	**- 70.4%**
Boeing	44.00	96.48	+ 119.3%
Caterpillar	25.97	75.51	+ 190.8%
CitiGroup	43.50	55.08	+ 26.6%
Coca Cola	61.06	51.48	**- 15.7%**
Disney	33.56	36.27	+ 8.1%
DuPont	67.39	52.04	**- 22.8%**
ExxonMobil	41.87	82.77	+ 97.7%
General Electric	50.33	37.34	**- 25.8%**
General Motors	82.25	31.36	**- 61.9%**
Hewlett Packard	56.25	45.58	**- 19.0%**
Home Depot	61.94	38.53	**- 37.8%**
Honeywell	59.87	56.98	**- 4.8%**
IBM	119.62	106.70	**- 10.8%**
Intel	51.53	22.99	**- 55.4%**
Johnson & Johnson	46.84	63.58	+ 35.7%
J P Morgan Chase	49.25	52.29	+ 6.2%
McDonalds	42.60	52.50	+ 23.2%
Merck	74.12	54.15	**- 26.9%**
Microsoft	56.12	30.69	**- 45.3%**
Minnesota Mining Mfg	49.65	87.06	+ 75.3%
Pfizer	37.0	27.37	**- 26.0%**
Proctor & Gamble	58.50	63.00	+ 7.7%
United Technologies	31.90	69.21	+ 117.0%
Verizon	56.31	42.61	**- 24.3%**
WalMart	64.50	46.54	**- 27.8%**

So, an investor *could* have outperformed the index by simply investing mostly in those six stocks, while avoiding the 24 other stocks in the index that did not do so well.

However, with 16 of those other stocks still down an average of 30% after 7 years, and 8 up only fractionally, the odds would obviously be stacked in favor of having a portfolio of losers, not the six big winners that carried the index to new highs.

But the dream continues that one can beat the market through superior stock or sector selection. It's a dream that does not go away no matter how many times through their investing lives investors are abused by it.

Yet even buying and holding an index fund is not easy.

Yes, buying and holding an index fund will eliminate individual stock risk, and sector risk, and will match the performance of the index, and therefore the market—*if you could stick with the strategy.*

An investor who owned an index fund on the Dow at the market peak in 2000, would have seen it decline 38.7% in the 2000-2002 bear market. But it would now have fully recovered and be 15.5% above its 2000 high. Not bad considering that most of the individual stocks in the Dow are still down an average of 30%, and the Nasdaq *Index* is still 50% below its bull market peak in 2000.

But as we discussed before, even the most determined buy and hold investor will not hold through bear market declines, and that is true even if they are holding an index fund. The financial and emotional pain is just too much to bear when one's life savings are disappearing 10%, 20%, 30% at a time. In the 2000-2002 bear market the Dow declined 38.7%, the S&P 500 lost 50% of its value, and the Nasdaq lost 78% of its value.

The majority of investors will bail out near the lows, after the damage is done, whether invested in diversified mutual funds, sector funds, individual stocks—or index funds.

However, do bear markets come along often enough to worry about? In 1999 and 2000 it was widely thought that bear markets were events of the past, which modern day investors would not see again in their lifetimes. The 2000-2002 bear market disabused them of that notion. But was the 2000-2002 bear market just a fluke?

Chapter 7

A Dangerous Myth—That Bear Markets Are Rare Events!

The rip-roaring bull market of the 1990s lasted for a record nine years. Its longevity, coupled with all the talk of it being 'a new era' in which the economy would continue to thrive for decades to come, had investors convinced that another bear market would not be seen in our lifetimes.

That unusual decade made investing seem so easy that it attracted new investors as no other bull market had ever done. High school and college investment clubs became the rage. Interest in the stock market became so widespread that specialized magazines previously devoted entirely to news, housekeeping, travel, beauty, entertainment, or what have you, began including sections on investing.

It all seemed so easy and profitable that by 1999 relatively inexperienced investors were quitting their jobs and careers to become full-time day-traders. For experienced investors it recalled the old market adage mentioned before, that "There is nothing like a bull market to make every investor think they are an investing genius."

How could the market's history be ignored by so many?

One factor was that a new generation of investors was in place. They had no scars from previous bear markets to remind them of how the market cycles back and forth so frequently between bull and bear markets. They knew only the excitement of how much had already been made by others in 1997 and 1998, and wanted in.

If they had even heard of the 1987 crash, they had probably also heard that the market recovered from it in less than a year. They were not aware of the fear the crash created at the time, and how the majority of investors, as always happens, had bailed out near the crash low with huge losses, and did not get back in until the market was back at its previous highs a year later.

They may have heard of the 1990 bear market, but not having lived through it either, blew that off as a non-event. After all, the decline had only lasted for three months. The S&P 500 had only declined 20.5%. The recovery had apparently been quite quick. The new investors were not aware that once again many had sold near the lows, pessimism having the consensus expectation at the time being that even lower prices lay ahead.

The new investors of the 1990s actually thought they had discovered a risk-free money-making machine, and it never breaks down in any serious way.

The stock market became the exciting topic of conversation around water coolers and over dinner tables. The profits were just so easy. Buy most any stock at any price and profits were assured. New issues coming to market were jumping 20%, 30%, 50% in their first month, sometimes their first week, of trading.

Eventually even former conservative investors were caught up in the excitement and confidence that bear markets were a thing of the past.

Wall Street was telling them they had it exactly right, that it was 'a new era', in which computers and automation made companies so efficient that corporate earnings would keep growing well into the next century. Economic recessions and stock market declines were events that had taken place back in the old days, back when the economy cycled back and forth between boom times and recessions, before the Federal Reserve learned how to keep everything on an even keel. In the new era, the stock market would just keep rising.

The mania carried many of the same code phrases and mantras that had passed as popular wisdom in every exciting bull market of the previous 200 years. It was a 'new era'. 'Stock valuations no longer matter'. Talk of caution, diversification, that a bear market was overdue, was 'dinosaur thinking'.

Investment books were being published by famous Wall Street figures telling investors all they had to do to choose good stocks was look around their homes and invest in companies whose products they liked.

So investors who liked the products of Disney, Home Depot, Circuit City, Microsoft, eBay, Outback Steakhouse, Yahoo and others, bought those stocks in 1999, even though they had already been popular stocks for years, had already tripled or quadrupled in price, and were selling at 40 or 50 or 80 times their earnings.

It was reminiscent of Japan's market top in 1989, when Japan's financial institutions were assuring Japanese housewives that they too could become wealthy from stock market investments. All they had to do was "put some of their monthly household budget" into the market.

The Beardstown Ladies, an investment club of fifteen elderly amateur investors meeting monthly in the basement of a church in a small town in Illinois, became famous. They reportedly were making large profits by competing directly with Wall Street professionals in analyzing the sales, products, and prospects of individual companies. They claimed it was easy, their profits produced by analysis that any amateur could utilize.

Only after they had written several best-selling books and made popular appearances on TV, was it discovered that they did not understand even the basics of calculating gains and losses. Their portfolio was growing primarily because they were contributing substantial amounts of new money to it each month, and counting that increase in assets as portfolio gains.

One of the most popular books of the time, published in September, 1999 was *Dow 36,000*, in which the authors predicted the DJIA, then approaching 11,000, was headed non-stop to 36,000. It became a best seller.

As an indication of how one-sided the thinking was at the time, my own book *Riding the Bear—How to Prosper in the Coming Bear Market*, also published in 1999, accurately predicting that the worst bear market since that of 1929-32 was right around the corner, sold only 20,000 copies.

Those who did read it raved about it, as could be seen in the readers' reviews posted on Amazon.com, where it was continuously ranked for several years with a rare unanimous Five Stars. I still receive letters from people saying, "The best investment book I've ever read. I just wish I had read it in time." "I don't know how you could have known so much about the investor frauds that were going on before they were revealed in the subsequent 2002 investigations."

Yet, the publisher could not get a single newspaper or financial magazine to even review it in 1999. It was apparently too preposterous for them to think that a bear market was right around the corner. Much more likely was Dow 36,000. Wall Street experts were telling them so.

Of course we know what happened. A few months after *Riding the Bear* came out, the record breaking 1990s bull market ended, and was indeed replaced by a serious three-year bear market—in which the S&P 500 lost 50% of its value, and the Nasdaq lost 78% of its value.

Rather than running up from 12,000 to 36,000, the DJIA instead tumbled to 7,200.

Subsequent investigations and scandals in 2002 revealed the very Wall Street scams, self-serving analysts' reports, and willfully misleading statements by Wall Street spokesmen and corporate managements that *Riding the Bear* warned about in 1999.

The firms paid many $billions in fines, and a few individuals served jail time. But has the situation really changed?

An important question is whether the 2000-2002 bear market was a rare event?

You need to realize that the only rare aspect about it was that it took so long to arrive. (The 1990s bull market was the longest lasting bull market in history, lasting nine years).

As the following table shows, the Dow experienced 24 bear markets between 1901 and 2000, an average of *one every 4.1 years*. The average decline was 35.7%. The ten largest declines averaged 48%, wiping out almost half of the stock market's value each time.

MARKET TOP	MARKET LOW	DECLINE	MARKET TOP	MARKET LOW	DECLINE
6-17-1901	11-9-1903	- 41%	9-12-1939	4-28-1942	- 40.4%
1-19-1906	11-15-1907	- 48.5%	5-29-1946	5-17-1947	- 23.2%
11-19-1909	9-25-1911	- 27.4%	4-6-1956	10-22-1957	- 20.0%
9-30-1912	7-30-1914	- 24.1%	12-13-1961	6-26-1962	- 27.1%
11-21-1916	12-19-1917	- 40.1%	2-9-1966	10-7-1966	- 25.2%
11-3-1919	8-24-1921	- 46.6%	12-3-1968	5-26-1970	- 35.9%
9-3-29	11-13-1929	- 47.9%	1-11-1973	12-6-1974	- 45.1%
4-17-30	7-8-1932	- 86.0%	9-21-1976	2-28-1978	- 26.9%
9-7-32	2-27-1933	- 37.2%	4-27-1981	8-12-1982	- 24.1%
2-5-1934	7-26-1934	- 22.8%	8-25-1987	10-19-1987	- 36.1%
3-10-1937	3-31-1938	- 49.1%	7-16-1990	10-11-1990	-21.2%
11-12-1938	4-8-1939	- 23.3%	1-14-2000	10-10-2002	- 38.7%
Average decline 35.7%. Ten largest declines averaged 48%.					

Further, they did not take place only in 'the old days'. In fact, from 1955, which is considered to be the beginning of the post-war modern market era, to 1990, a period of 35 years, there were 10 bear markets, or one on average of every 3.5 years.

The broader-based S&P 500 Index, which came into being much later than the Dow, has experienced similar bear markets.

Market Top	Bear Market Low	Decline
1-11-1973	10-4-1974	- 50.0%
9-22-76	3-1-1978	- 20.4%
11-26-1980	8-12-1982	- 28.3%
8-25-1987	10-20-1987	- 35.6%
7-16-1990	10-11-1990	- 20.1%
3-24-2000	10-10-2002	- 50.4%
Average decline 34%		

We're obviously talking about significant declines, on average of every three or four years, devastating intervals for investors who do not expect them, or know how to handle them.

• It is primarily bear markets that account for the dismal statistic that 80% of investors either lose money in the stock market over the long term, or fail to match the gain they would make by simply leaving their money in the bank.

The DJIA and S&P 500 consist of the largest, strongest, most conservative stocks available. Many, if not most, individual investors have little interest in conservative stocks. They invest chiefly in the more speculative issues of the Nasdaq, the home of the most exciting stocks. So we must look at the Nasdaq to more accurately see the problems most investors run into with bear markets.

NASDAQ Performance in Bear Markets Since its Inception.

Market Top	Bear Market Low	Decline
1-11-1973	10-3-1974	- 60.0%
9-13-1978	11-14-1978	- 20.3%
5-29-1981	8-16-1982	- 28.5%
8-17-1987	10-28-1987	- 36.1%
10-10-1989	10-12-1990	-33.8%
7-21-1998	10-8-1998	- 33.1%
3-10-2000	10-10-2002	- 77.6%
Average decline 41.4%		

The Nasdaq's average declines in bear markets have been 41.4%, compared to 35.7% for the DJIA, and 34% for the S&P 500.

However, even that statistic does not reveal all of the additional risk of buy and hold investing in Nasdaq stocks.

Since the Nasdaq's inception in 1971, the DJIA and S&P 500 experienced 'only' six bear markets, while as the table shows, the Nasdaq experienced seven. That came about because in 1998 the U.S. stock market plunged sharply in reaction to collapses in Asian markets (brought on by a crisis in Asian currencies). In that plunge the DJIA and S&P 500 declined only 19.3%, not quite reaching the minimum 20% decline that is the official definition of a bear market. However, the Nasdaq plunged 33.1%.

THE UPSIDE POTENTIAL OF NASDAQ INVESTING

On the bright side, the Nasdaq also has greater volatility on the upside, rising faster than the more conservative indexes in bull markets.

For example, in the current bull market, which began in 2002, the DJIA gained 71% from its low in 2002 to the end of 2006. The S&P 500 gained 83% during the same period. The Nasdaq however gained a huge 168%.

Therefore, you might wonder if the Nasdaq's larger gains in bull markets is enough to offset its larger declines in bear markets, perhaps making buying and holding of the Nasdaq over the long-term a viable strategy.

The answer can be seen in the next table. It compares the three major indexes over the last 9 years. Those 9 years included the last two years of the 1990s bull market, the subsequent three-year bear market, and then four years of the new bull market that began in 2002.

That provides a decided bias in favor of the Nasdaq, since it includes six years of bull market when the Nasdaq tends to out-perform, and only three years of bear market when the Nasdaq tends to under-perform.

And yet over the entire cycle, the Nasdaq under-performed the Dow and S&P 500 to a significant degree.

Year	DJIA	S&P 500	NASDAQ
1998 (Bull Market)	+ 17.9%	+ 28.0%	+ 39.6%
1999 (Bull Market)	+ 26.8%	+ 20.1%	+ 85.6%
2000 (Bear Market)	- 4.6%	- 9.1%	- 39.3%
2001 (Bear Market)	- 5.3%	- 11.9%	- 21.1%

2002 (Bear Market)	- 14.7%	- 22.1%	- 31.5%
2003 (Bull Market)	+ 27.6%	+ 28.7%	+ 50.0%
2004 (Bull Market)	+ 5.5%	+ 10.9%	+ 8.6%
2005 (Bull Market)	+ 1.6%	+ 4.8%	+ 1.4%
2006 (Bull Market)	+ 18.5%	+ 15.4%	+ 9.5%
9- Year Total Return	+ 86.3%	+ 65.5%	+ 53.7%

Note: These are 'total returns' including the dividends paid each year by the stocks that were in the indexes at the time.

Yes, the NASDAQ did tend to make much larger gains in bull markets than did the Dow and S&P 500. However, in spite of huge gains of 85.6% in 1999, and 50% in 2003, the NASDAQ still failed to match the performance of the DJIA or S&P 500 Index over the full cycle of bull and bear markets.

Keep in mind also that to even achieve that 9-year gain of 53.7%, a buy and hold investor in the Nasdaq would have had to handle the stress of it losing 78% from its 2000 peak to its 2002 trough, *and still being 50% below its 2000 peak seven years later, in 2007.*

Summing up what we have learned so far:

- Investors have little hope of competing head-to-head on the same playing field with experienced, well-equipped, Wall Street professionals and institutions.

- Statistics show that the most popular approaches, resorting to tips from Wall Street and well-meaning friends, and 'chasing performance', do not work.

- Depending on good mutual fund managers to provide market-beating gains is unlikely to be satisfactory, since the majority of even the best managers fail to match the market indexes over the long term.

- Buy and hold investing is not a viable strategy because it is next to impossible to simply "pick good stocks and hold them for the very long term". Very few, if any 'long-term' stocks exist.

- The myth of buy and hold investing cannot even be supported by the promise that "the market always comes back". It can take decades for the market indexes to come back.

- When the indexes do eventually come back they have undergone dramatic changes, to include the newest strong companies. They do not represent the same 'market' that went away.

- Remaining invested on a buy and hold basis during U.S. bear markets prevents investors from taking advantage of positive moves that may be taking place in other markets.

- Wall Street firms, mutual funds, hedge funds, corporate insiders, successful private investors, do not buy and hold with their own money

- Bear markets are not rare events. Except for the 1920s and 1990s, one has taken place on average of every 3.9 years.

- Investors are attracted to the NASDAQ for very good reason. It makes much greater gains in bull markets. *However*, it suffers much larger losses in market downturns.

So what does work?

If buy and hold investing does not work, cannot work, what are the alternatives?

Think about it! There are only two alternatives.

- One can decide not to invest in the stock market at all, and miss out on the most viable investing venue available, better than bonds, gold, collectibles, and yes, even real estate.

- Or one can engage in some type of market-timing.

I can hear the collective gasp. "But Wall Street tells us the market cannot be timed."

The interesting thing about the situation is that, as discussed before, in direct contrast to their advice to public investors, virtually all professionals, including mutual funds, hedge funds, brokerage firms, money-managers, corporate insiders, and large individual investors (including Warren Buffett) depend on market-timing for the major portion of their success.

- And virtually all individual investors, even those who consider themselves to be determined buy and hold investors, eventually become market-timers, *but with the worst of timing,* by bailing out in disgust near the lows.

So let's forget what Wall Street says about market-timing for the moment, and look into it with an open mind.

Chapter 8

Market-Timing!

You will often hear analysts and investors complain that the stock market is not rational. That is, the market hardly ever does what analysis of surrounding economic, political, or fundamental conditions indicates that it *should* do. Or as the old Wall Street maxim says;

"The market does whatever it must to fool the majority of investors."

That is because the stock market is forward-looking. It anticipates what economic conditions will be six months to a year out, while the 'crowd' bases its bullishness or bearishness on its *feelings* about *current* conditions.

Even those who focus on analysis of economic reports as perhaps a better indication than 'feelings' about current conditions, run into a problem. Government and other agencies must wait for data to come in before they can compile the economic reports that dominate the financial media. So we receive this quarter the economic report on how much the economy grew, or failed to grow, in the previous quarter. We receive this month the report on the level of consumer spending or inflation that took place two months ago.

The problem has been described as 'investing through the rearview mirror'.

Thus does the market top out when the majority least expect it, when current conditions are great, when the economy is booming along, employment is strong, and corporations are making good profits.

What happens is that at some point so-called 'smart money', meaning Wall Street institutions, corporate insiders and the like, begin thinking current economic growth has become unsustainable. Perhaps the labor market has become 'tight', or interest rates have risen, or consumers have become overloaded with debt. They believe those problems will lead to the economy and corporate earnings being in trouble six months to a year in the future.

So, even as economic reports covering *previous* quarters or months continue to come in positive, and *current* conditions remain great, the smart money begins selling.

That initial selling activity is not easy to discern. Perhaps statistics show heavy insider selling, combined with deteriorating market 'internals' as more stocks close down than up each week, even as the narrow market indexes continue to make gains.

As the 'smart money' begins to quietly sell, more investors, primarily professional managers who have contacts with the 'smart money', join in the selling, taking their profits while the market is still rising rather than risk having to sell into a declining market. (As such famous investors as Joseph P. Kennedy and Bernard Baruch pointed out in a previous era, and others, including Warren Buffett, of the current era have said, they would rather be early, leaving some profit on the table, than risk being too late).

At the opposite end of the cycle, as the stock market approaches its next important bottom, surrounding conditions are always terrible and getting worse.

That is also understandable. There has been a serious market correction to reach that market low, perhaps even a bear market. It handed investors losses that caused them to bail out of most of their holdings.

The poor economic conditions that the 'smart money' anticipated when they sold near the market top have arrived. Economic growth is slowing. Corporate earnings are declining. The slowing economy has unemployment rising. High levels of consumer, corporate, or federal debt, which had been ignored when the economy was booming along, suddenly look like serious problems. The majority of investors now believe there is no possibility of the market decline ending anytime soon. The trend, which is now down, is being extended endlessly into the future.

However, at some point in the midst of the gloom, 'smart money', again looking ahead rather than through the side window, begins to anticipate conditions won't get any worse. They begin nibbling at stocks again. As they become more convinced that economic conditions will be improving six months to a year ahead, they begin to load up on stocks.

Perhaps they see signs that Congress will begin providing economic stimulus in the form of increased federal spending, or that the Federal Reserve might be getting ready to cut interest rates. Whatever it is they see, having taken their profits at the previous top, perhaps making more profits by positioning for the downside prior to the market's decline, they now begin buying, and the market begins to rise.

However, the majority of non-professional investors, having been burned each time they bought the previous dips on the way down, are having nothing to do with it. No way could this be the bottom. They will not lose their pessimism until the better conditions smart money is anticipating have already shown up, six months to a year later. By then most of the easy money has been made in the new bull market.

Thus does investor sentiment cycle between greed and fear, reaching the extremes of both conditions at exactly the wrong time.

- Statistics show that *every* market top has always been accompanied by excessive bullishness and reckless public buying. Conversely, *every* important bottom has always been accompanied by excessive fear, bearishness, and lack of interest in the market.

An example that should still be vivid in the minds of most investors is the market's reaction after the terrorist attacks of September 11, 2001.

At the time, the economy was already mired in the 2001 recession. The stock market was in the midst of the severe 2000-2002 bear market. Consumer and investor sentiment was very negative and pessimistic. The DJIA had topped out at 11,723 in early 2000 and had declined to 9,605 by September 10, 2001, the day before the terrorist attacks. The Nasdaq, which had topped out in 2000 at 5,078, had plunged 72%, all the way to 1,423. The consensus opinion was that the market was headed much lower, that in fact there was no bottom in sight.

Then a nightmare that could not have been imagined was added to the fear and pessimism. The frightening terrorist attacks on New York and Washington took place.

New York, and particularly its financial district, was hit hard. The stock exchanges were closed for a week. Investors could not sell to move to the sidelines even if they wanted to. Airlines across the country were grounded. More attacks were expected at any time. Shopping malls and theatres were deserted as Americans hunkered in their homes.

Political, military, and economic experts studied the facts and issued reports and projections. There was complete agreement. The majority expectation was that America would never be the same again. Its population was destined to spend the next several decades living in fear, afraid to venture far from home, hunkered down and hoarding food and cash. Its already declining economy would collapse further, probably into a repeat of the Great Depression of the 1930s. The stock market would crash further, with the Dow possibly plunging to less than 1,000.

Instead, when the exchanges re-opened a week later, the stock market declined for only another five days. Then, contrary to the popular expectations, the market launched into a substantial rally. As shown in the following chart, rather than plunging to less than 1000, the DJIA surged up 29% to 10,632 by March 22, 2002. The always more volatile Nasdaq rose a huge 45%.

The severe bear market would not end until October, 2002, and at a lower low. But it was a powerful rally within the 2000-2002 bear market, a so-called bear market rally. And it began precisely when pessimism was at an extreme, when analysis of current conditions could hardly have made the future look bleaker.

The 'smart money', as usual, was not looking at the current

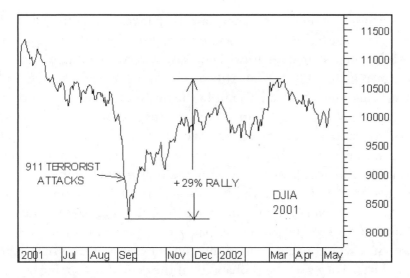

911 TERRORIST
ATTACKS

+29% RALLY

DJIA
2001

situation, which was made even more grim by the terrorist attacks. Smart money was looking six months to a year ahead, anticipating (correctly) that the government would step in with efforts that would re-stimulate the economy.

As an example of what happens at the other end of the investor sentiment cycle, one has only to recall the optimistic, euphoric conditions in place at the important stock market top in 2000. Spirits could not have been higher. Investors, political leaders, and the general public were convinced the strong economy, and therefore the 1990s bull market, would last for many more years. They had only to look out the side window at the strong consumer and corporate spending, high employment, even Federal budget surpluses, to be convinced of that.

But 'smart money' began selling heavily, taking their big profits from the long bull market. The stock market bubble burst. The devastating decline into the 2000-2002 bear market began.

What did 'smart money' see that the majority were either unaware of, or chose to ignore?

They saw the situations I was warning about at the time in my 1999 book, *Riding the Bear—How To Prosper in the Coming Bear Market.*

Among other things, they saw that investor 'sentiment' had reached, and exceeded, the extreme of bullishness and euphoria usually seen at market tops. They saw investor buying of stocks on margin (credit) was at a record high, an indication investors were running out of cash to put in the market to keep stock prices rising. They saw a stock market that was extremely overbought, and stocks that were extremely overvalued, selling at 30, 40, and 50 times earnings. They saw investors not caring what prices they paid, so convinced were they that the bull market would run on endlessly. Yet they saw the Federal Reserve raising interest rates to slow the over-heated economy before it could cause runaway inflation. Corporate insiders in particular knew that higher interest rates would make it more difficult for consumers to buy their products. They saw the probability of the economy topping out in six months to a year, perhaps slowing all the way into recession.

And sure enough, a year or so after the market topped out into the very serious 2000-2002 bear market, the economy was in the midst of the 2001 recession.

- It is for good reason then that successful market-timing concentrates on methods of avoiding 'crowd think', even sometimes uses the majority opinion at the time as a 'contrary indicator'.

However, although thinking and acting opposite to majority opinion at market tops and bottoms is vitally important, and is critical to investing success, it is not easy.

Obviously the popular opinion is going to dominate financial publications and TV interviews of Wall Street representatives. Whatever is the majority, or popular opinion is also certainly going to be the view of friends and acquaintances, and dominate conversations.

How can one not be influenced by so much one-sided evidence and advice coming from all directions, particularly since it seems so right because the market is still going up?

The first requirement is to;

THINK CYCLES NOT ENDLESS TRENDS.

The favorite forecasting tool of scientists and economists, as well as investors, is to extend current trends in a straight line endlessly into the future.

Mark Twain made fun of the tendency in *Life on the Mississippi.*

The Mississippi River meanders in great loops around sand bars. Twain noted that the force of the river under flood conditions allowed it to sometimes take a short cut across a sand bar, with the short-cut widening and eventually becoming the main course of the river in that area. Twain noted that thus had the river been shortening its route by an average of just over a mile per year for a number of years. Tongue in cheek, he extended that trend into the future, noting that "Any person can see that seven hundred and forty-two years from now the Lower Mississippi will be only a mile and three-quarters long."

I like to say that the fallacy of extending trends in a straight line into the future is illustrated by the fact that the world hardly ever comes to an end. Yet for centuries 'trend-extending' has regularly predicted such an outcome—based on everything from holy wars and black plague, nuclear warfare, depletion of the ozone layer, global warming, and communism taking over the world, to fears of an AIDS pandemic, SARS, and bird-flu pandemics.

In the 1940s, it was scientific fact that by the year 2000, there would not be enough land to feed the growing U.S. population. Large scale starvation would have the country in ruins. Statistics were completely supportive of the projection. It took a fixed amount of land to grow enough food and support enough livestock, to feed a given number of people. The population was growing at a fast pace, while land was actually being taken out of agriculture to provide housing space for that growing population.

By simply extending the line of population growth, and the decline of available farm land, the result was inevitable. By the year 2000 the U.S. population would be reduced to hungry masses living in conditions similar to those in undeveloped countries.

However, trends continue only until conditions change.

Farmers learned new soil management, new cattle-feeding and breeding techniques. Science developed healthier seeds. Farm machinery manufacturers provided more efficient equipment. Oblivion was not only avoided and the trend reversed, but the pendulum swung to the opposite extreme, of food surpluses and overflowing government food warehouses. By the 1970s the U.S. government was even making gifts of surplus grains to foreign countries, and providing subsidies to farmers to leave their fields unplanted.

Think cycles not endless trends.

Cures are discovered for the most devastating of diseases. The result is that the straight-line trend to extinction is not only halted, but reversed to ever-longer life expectancies.

Not surprisingly, that new trend is then extended in a straight line in the opposite direction. Fears arise that ever longer life-expectancies will bankrupt the Social Security system. Ever older but healthier elders, taking from society but no longer contributing, will eventually pull the economy down into a permanent recession.

Communism spreads around half the planet, raising a real concern that it will eventually take over the rest of the world. But in the process it stretches its untenable economics past the tipping point, and the trend reverses to the present expectation that communism is history.

But, don't bet on that trend lasting forever either, given the current drift of the rich getting richer and the poor getting poorer. In third world countries that will eventually create uprisings again, and revolutions that will promise to re-distribute wealth. Already in recent months, leftist candidates have won presidential elections in Argentina, Bolivia, Brazil, Chile, Venezuela, and Uruguay. Leftist Evo Morales, who twice participated in popular street uprisings against Bolivia's ruling elite, won Bolivia's election, and vowed his leftist "Movement Toward Socialism" will "change history".

GOVERNMENTS LOVE EXTENDING CURRENT TRENDS.

Governments are certainly not immune to the fallacy of thinking trends rather than cycles.

In the 1980s, the U.S. budget deficit had been worsening for several decades. Economists, extending the trend in a straight line into the future, competed with each other with dire forecasts of how soon the country would be bankrupt.

However, in the 1990s, government spending cut-backs, combined with a big surge in tax revenues (thanks to the booming economy and explosive stock market of the 1990s), not only produced a balanced budget, but several years of large budget *surpluses*.

Not surprisingly, in no time at all, *that* trend was being extended endlessly into the future. Congress began making plans to spend the budget surpluses it was now projecting would continue for several decades.

Washington projected that within ten years the entire U.S. national debt would be paid off; social security would be completely funded; and the population could be provided with full healthcare. There would even be plenty left over for tax cuts, and increased spending for defense and education.

Once again the trend only lasted until conditions changed. The stock market plunged into the severe 2000-2002 bear market, depriving the government of the healthy capital gains taxes it had been receiving. The economy plunged into the 2001 recession. Workers lost their jobs, causing the government's take from income taxes to nose-dive. The 911 terrorist attacks took place, resulting in large increases in government spending for homeland security. The invasion of Iraq followed, with its escalating costs. The picture reversed again. Budget surpluses became budget deficits.

Not surprisingly, as the budget deficits have reached record levels, economists are now extending *that* trend in a straight line again into the future, returning to predictions that the Social Security system will soon be bankrupt, the country will face dire healthcare shortfalls for decades, and providing school and welfare funding will be an insurmountable problem.

And so it goes, cycle after cycle, as conditions swing back and forth from one extreme to the other. Sometimes the pendulum catches a tailwind, and a trend lasts longer than usual. But at some point, the pendulum reaches an extreme and begins to swing in the opposite direction.

Nowhere is the tendency to extend trends in a straight line, without expectations of reversal, more prevalent than in the world of finance, economics, and investing.

When a rising trend is underway in the stock market, such as in the late 1990s, and surrounding conditions continue to look wonderful, the expectation becomes that the rising trend need never end. Thus a bull market that has resulted in the Dow rising from 6,000 to 12,000 is extended in the minds of investors (and book authors) in an uninterrupted straight line to 36,000.

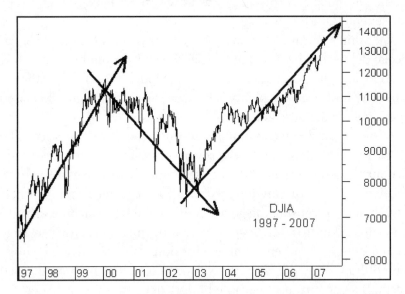

When it instead ends (because 'smart money' looks ahead and sees that conditions will be different a year or so in the future) the 'crowd', or majority, is at first disbelieving, still looking out the side window, still seeing that everything remains positive. They even compound their error by buying the market's dips.

However, once it becomes obvious and undeniable that the

trend is to the downside, *that* trend is then extended in a straight line into the future. The popular thought then becomes that conditions can only get worse.

- Thus do most investors get caught every time, extending the trend of great conditions that are in place at every market top, and then later extending endlessly into the future the terrible conditions in place at every market bottom.

It may seem therefore that an investor only needs to watch investor sentiment, sell when 'the crowd' becomes overly bullish, buy back when the crowd becomes excessively bearish.

However, investor sentiment is not that precise. The degree of extreme optimism and bullishness at market tops, and pessimism and bearishness at market bottoms, varies from cycle to cycle.

Therefore investor sentiment can only be used as a 'gauge of risk' that a change in trend *may* be approaching.

When investor sentiment approaches an extreme of either bullishness near market tops, or bearishness near market bottoms, most successful market-timing relies on the use of 'technical' analysis to provide the actual 'signals' that trend reversals are taking place.

TECHNICAL ANALYSIS

The beauty of technical analysis is that it is completely mechanical. It focuses on what the market is doing, not what current conditions, or even 'looking ahead' analysis, says it *should* be doing.

It measures whether money is flowing into the market, or out, regardless of the reason. It measures whether a trend remains in place or is reversing, regardless of what careful analysis of conditions says it should be doing.

Thus it avoids the human emotions of greed or fear that influence most investors at precisely the wrong time in the cycles. Technical analysis, being mechanical measurements of what the market is doing, is not even aware of the surrounding conditions that may be creating the extreme bullish or bearish emotions of investors at the time.

Until 1950, technical analysis was practiced by few, and was considered by those who had not looked into it, as some kind of unfathomable hocus-pocus. However, it increasingly proved its value, particularly after the introduction of computers allowed easier accumulation and analysis of data.

Technical analysis now plays an important part in the approach of most professional and serious investors, even those expecting to buy and hold once they have made their investment selections.

Yet, while all Wall Street institutions and money-management firms utilize technical analysis to at least the same degree as fundamental analysis, one would never know that from their presentations to the public.

Publicly they base projections for the future performance of a stock solely on the fundamentals of the company's products, sales and earnings trends, and the competency of its management. Similarly, projections for the future direction of the overall market are invariably based on interest rates, inflation, the employment picture, corporate earnings, and other basic fundamental situations the public can easily understand.

There's a reason for that.

If Wall Street spoke of how the charts of a stock are showing a 'pick-up in big block accumulation on pull-backs to support at a rising 20-week moving average', or 'a pattern of higher highs on each rally off the support', or 'higher volume on the rallies and lower volume on the pull-backs', eyes would glaze over. Few non-professional listeners would understand what they were talking about, much less see those factors as signs of a potential rally or a damaging decline coming in a stock, sector, or the overall market.

However, if they speak of exciting products, or good management, or rising sales or earnings, that kind of talk is easily understood by everyone. It makes for an easier sell of a stock or sector, or the opinion that they have about the overall market.

It's not a new situation.

A prominent brokerage firm partner in the 1920s, Richard D. Wyckoff, recounted in his memoirs how he chose stocks for his clients primarily using technical analysis. But when his technical analysis turned up a stock he wanted to recommend, he then had to uncover the fundamental conditions that sounded good and supported the buy signal that had been triggered via technical analysis. Only by converting his technical reasons for being bullish or bearish on a stock into the kind of talk about the company's products or sales that the clients were used to, could he get them to accept his recommendations.

THE ORIGINAL TECHNICAL ANALYST.

While we're talking about the old days, the story of one of the first investors to trade on technical analysis and charting alone, without *any* regard at all for a company's fundamentals, is interesting, as well as revealing.

In books and interviews Jesse Livermore, the famed stock market operator of the early 1900s, described his discovery of technical analysis.

In the early days, brokerage firms hired 'board boys' to mark the changing prices of stocks on the 'big board' in the lobby of their firms. Their customers would gather there to watch the day's market activity. At the age of 14 Livermore was one of those 'board boys' in a small regional brokerage firm outside of New York.

He wasn't on the job long before he noticed that some stocks seemed to make big moves immediately after a change showed up in the trading volume of the stock. He began keeping notes and tracking those daily volume and price patterns. He said most often he didn't even know what a company's business or product was, sometimes not even its name but only its stock symbol. However, by simply watching the way its stock was trading he seemed to often be able to determine when it was going to make a move in one direction or the other.

After several months of tracking such activity, Livermore was satisfied that he had made an important discovery. He borrowed $5 from a friend to test his theory. Within months, at the age of 15, he had used his tape-watching technique to run that $5 into $1,000, the equivalent of $20,000 in today's dollars. By the time he was

21 he had increased his portfolio another tenfold, to $10,000 (the equivalent of $200,000 today). He then moved to New York to become a full-time trader.

From that $5 beginning, he went on to become a famous multi-millionaire investor, known as the 'Wall Street Wonder', blamed by some for the 1929 stock market crash, with a large staff of 'technical analysts' trained to help him track trading patterns.

Early on he surmised the changes in large block trading volume he was tracking signaled that large investors and institutions (smart money?) were quietly accumulating or distributing stock. He theorized that meant something was happening that other investors were not yet aware of, which would cause the stock to make a significant move once the information was made public.

He also soon became aware of how the 'crowd', by its actions, often signaled the market was near a top or bottom. Of one particular period just after he had returned from an extended vacation in Europe, Livermore said, "I almost immediately ran into the beginning of a bull market, and over the next two years my stake grew substantially. But then the public got wind of it [the bull market], and went stock mad. I knew the end was near."

He was right. Several months later, the stock market collapsed so fast that of the situation Livermore said;

> *"The price collapses were just awful. The trading floor was way behind the sell orders, and the tape was running so far behind the transactions, that a seller had no way of knowing at what price he was selling. A stock that closed at $100 the previous day, opened at $80 the next morning. If an investor then put in an order to sell, by the time the order reached the trading floor and worked its way through the backlog of sell orders, the price was $60."*

The modern market had a similar experience in the October, 1987 crash!

The stock market had already been in a decline for three months when October, 1987 arrived, so bullish spirits had already been dampened. When the market began to plunge precipitously on October 19, panic set in, and the market was soon out of control. Sell orders so swamped the trading floor from the open that the NYSE was unable to find enough matching buyers to get all thirty Dow stocks open for trading until two hours into the session. By that time the Dow was already down nine percent. There was so much one-sided selling that trading in many stocks was repeatedly halted when at times there were no buyers *at any price*. So many panicked investors were trying to call their brokers to find out what was happening that phone lines were completely jammed. Those who had bought on margin discovered later that their holdings had been sold out near the lows when their brokers couldn't get through to them to issue a margin call.

And that was in the modern market, just twenty years ago. It is knowing the market's history of such events that prompts Wall Street institutions, corporate insiders, and sophisticated private investors to prefer to sell early, while the market is still rising, rather than wait until everyone is trying to crowd through the exit at the same time.

To repeat one of Warren Buffet's pieces of wisdom mentioned in an earlier chapter;

- "At the start of the party the punch is flowing and everything's going well, but you know at midnight it's all going to turn into pumpkins and mice. People think they'll be able to get out just before midnight, but everyone else thinks that too."

MODERN TECHNICAL ANALYSIS.

Technical analysis has changed significantly since Livermore's time, especially with the introduction of computers to accumulate and analyze data.

In broad terms, technical analysis can be broken down into several areas which combine to provide indications of risk, and even trigger buy and sell 'signals'. Those areas include

- **Chart analysis**

- Investor sentiment measurements
- Valuation levels
- Seasonality.

Chapter 9

Chart Analysis

It is not the goal or purpose of this book to teach chart analysis, or even delve deeply into it. The methods of market-timing I advocate simply do not require it.

However, a brief look at the tools of technical analysis will serve to illustrate how the market, and individual stocks and mutual funds, move through their cycles.

And that understanding is of great importance no matter what strategy an investor employs. It is of importance even to an investor who intends to buy and hold, since no matter the strategy, buying low and selling high is still the key to success.

Charts provide a broad array of information about a stock or a market in a very efficient manner, including its historical performance, its current trend, location of potential overhead resistance (where trends may reverse to the downside), and areas of potential support (which may bring an end to a downtrend).

As an example, the following chart shows the Dow and its relationship to its 200-day moving average (m.a.). Note how the m.a. acts as a magnet. Any time the Dow strays too far either above or below it, it eventually returns to the m.a.

I have marked with an A the occasions in the past when the Dow became 'over-extended' *above* its 200-day m.a. And I have drawn a trendline through the lows of the market corrections in 2004, 2005, and 2006 as a line of likely downside support for corrections as long as the bull market continues.

The chart tells us that when the DJIA becomes over-extended (overbought) above its 200-day m.a. the market is in danger of topping out into a serious correction of that overbought condition.

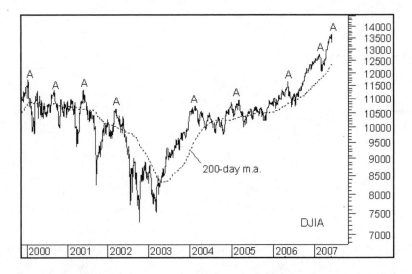

Note how often those conditions coincided with major market tops, as in January, 2000, and at the tops of the bear market rallies in late 2000, in 2001, and 2002. Even in the new bull market that began in 2002, similar overbought conditions above the 200-day moving average coincided with the beginning of intermediate-term corrections within the bull market.

Such a simple chart, yet it warned an investor when the time had arrived to become less confident about a market rally, and more willing to take profits.

Once a correction begins, the pendulum almost always then swings to the opposite extreme. That is, once such a correction begins it usually doesn't end until the Dow is over-extended *beneath* its 200-day m.a. to at least the same degree it had previously been overbought above it.

Therefore, the goal of chart analysis is simply to watch how the market or an individual stock or mutual fund is moving toward an overbought condition in a rally. If that overbought condition seems to be halting the market's rally, the market-technician then watches other technical 'indicators' to determine if money flow and momentum reverses enough to indicate the trend is reversing direction.

In the other direction, when the DJIA reaches an oversold condition by being extended *beneath* its 200-day moving average, or in a bull market by declining down to a potential support trendline, and its decline seems to be halting, the technician again looks to other technical 'indicators' to determine if money flow and momentum reverses enough to indicate *that* trend is reversing direction, that a new buying opportunity has arrived.

Obviously such charts and 'technical indications' are entirely mechanical and non-emotional. They are measurements of what the market is actually doing, not what 'the crowd' thinks it *should* be doing. Their importance is therefore obvious.

MOST INVESTORS ARE UNFAMILIAR WITH CHARTS.

Most investors know nothing of charts, technical analysis, or cycles. They simply buy or sell stocks and mutual funds based on tips and stories related to a company's products, and the *current* economic conditions.

One of my first indications of just how unfamiliar stock charts are to most investors came about in 1995.

The owner of a security alarm business had a small crew in our offices upgrading our alarm system. Aware that we were in some type of investment business, he was trying to pick our brains for investment advice.

For three years he had been pouring his business profits into mutual funds and was unhappy with their performance. His financial advisors had told him to expect an average annual return of 12% on his investments, and they weren't coming close.

I explained to him that the previous few years, the period between 1991 and 1994, had been very flat years for the market, and that it was very difficult to make large profits in a 'flat' market. He didn't understand. He explained again that every financial planner he had spoken with had provided him with similar projections and promises; that the stock market rises 12% per year. They expected to provide him with a mix of stocks and mutual funds that would produce at least that rate of return.

I explained that they were no doubt referring to the market's *average* annual return, that the market doesn't provide that kind of return every year, but does so, on average, over the long-term. Some years it's up much more than that, perhaps as much as 30%, while other years it has losses, also of perhaps as much as 30%.

He couldn't fathom that. (The 2000-2002 bear market was still a few years away, and the 1990s bull market had been underway since he had begun investing three years earlier). He was convinced he had been told he would make at least 12% a year, period.

There happened to be a six-foot framed chart of the Dow from 1900 through 1994 hanging on our conference room wall, and I led him to it. I showed him how over the very long-term the market's trend has always been to the upside. But there were periods such as he had just been through when the market was very flat for several years, producing very little in the way of gains. I pointed out the bear markets that had come along every few years, where his stocks or mutual funds might even decline 30 or 40%, and how often it had taken years for the market to return to its previous levels after such declines.

He was actually stunned, completely blown away. It was a reminder to me of how investors, busy in their own careers, are often unaware of how investing in the stock market works, even as they are participating in it with hard-earned money.

It was also a good lesson of how important it is for all investors to be familiar enough with charts to realize how stocks, mutual funds, and the overall market, move in cycles and patterns, not endless trends.

Today's investors are somewhat more familiar with charts, at least aware that they exist, than my friend in 1995. Exposure to financial TV shows, where charts are frequently employed, has helped in that regard. The 2000-2002 bear market should have also made the current generation of investors well aware of the market's ability to move in both directions.

However, few investors are aware of how charts can help them *anticipate* the market's moves before they take place.

In the previous chart I showed you how a long-term 200-day moving average can tell an investor when the market has become 'overbought' and therefore in danger of rolling over to the downside into a serious correction of that overbought condition.

Other moving averages and technical indicators can provide similar information on the probable direction of the market's short-term, and intermediate-term moves.

SHORT-TERM MOVING AVERAGES.

Moving averages smooth out the market's daily and weekly up and down fluctuations, making the direction of the trend more obvious.

The following chart shows how a 21-day moving average helps traders by smoothing out the ups and downs of the S&P 500. It allows traders to more clearly identify whether the S&P 500 is in a short-term rally or a short-term correction.

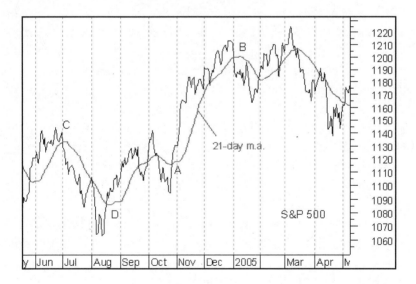

As the chart shows, from June, 2004, at the point marked C on the chart, until May 2005, for almost a year, the S&P 500 made little progress for a buy and hold investor, even though the market was in the bull market that began in 2002. The S&P 500 was at 1,140

at point C, and at 1,175 in May of the following year, a gain of just 1%.

However, *within that period* it had several more meaningful moves, its largest being a 15% gain from its low in August of 2004 to its high in March of 2005.

A *short-term* market-timer (trader) might use the 21-day moving average (m.a.) to help identify the short-term trend. Note how the moving average acts like a magnet, pulling the S&P 500 Index back to it when the index gets either too 'overbought' above the m.a., or too 'oversold' beneath the m.a. Thus it usually provides 'support' on brief pull-backs if a rally is to continue. In short-term corrections it will often be overhead 'resistance' that will stop rally attempts if the correction is to continue.

Only if the index moves through the moving average does the trader expect the short-term trend may be changing.

Thus a short-term trader using the 21-day moving average as a guide, might buy the S&P 500 index when the index has been in a correction, and then breaks out above its 21-day m.a, such as at point A in the chart. He would then take his profits from the trade when the index breaks back below the m.a., as at point B on the chart.

If the trader is also interested in going after gains from the downside, he might sell the S&P 500 index short when it breaks below the 21-day m.a., as at point C in the chart, and then take the profit when the index breaks back above the 21-day m.a., as at point D.

As the chart shows, not all such trades will produce a profit. Thus short-term traders are busy people, and to be successful must be disciplined in following the trading rule to "Cut losing trades quickly and let winning trades run".

A moving average can also help a longer-term investor stay in the market and not panic out on one of the market's periodic short-term declines.

For instance, beginning in August, 2006 there were a number of economic negatives in the news including the bursting of the real estate 'bubble', slowing economic growth, an inverted yield curve, etc. The bull market that began in 2002 was already the third longest-lasting bull market in history. Analysts were warning that a fairly serious correction could begin at any time.

However, as shown in the next chart, a 30-day moving average on the S&P 500 would have helped an investor remain invested throughout the period.

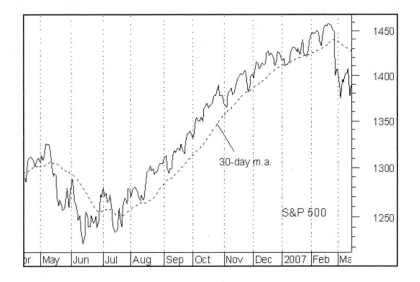

Each of the short-term pullbacks that took place had investors worried that a correction might have begun. That worry was enhanced by the fact that the new bull market had been somewhat strange, having gone for one of the longest periods ever without even a normal 10% to 15% correction. However, an investor watching a chart like this could see that the S&P 500 had been finding support at its 30-day moving average on each pullback, and then resumed its uptrend. As long as that continued to happen, the rally remained in effect. It was only later, in February, 2007, when the S&P pulled back to the moving average yet again, and did not find support there, but continued lower, that the chart produced a warning that a correction may have been unfolding.

LONGER–TERM MOVING AVERAGES.

Longer-term moving averages are useful for measuring intermediate-term trends. In the following chart I have applied a 20-*week*
m.a. to the S&P 500 index to illustrate how it defines intermediate-
term moves of several months to more than a year.

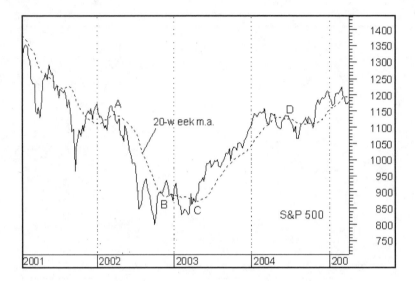

An intermediate-term trader might sell the S&P 500 index short
when it breaks below its 20-week m.a., as at point A on the chart,
and take the profit several months later when the index breaks
back above the m.a., as at point B. Likewise, he might buy the
index when, after a decline it reverses to the upside and crosses
above its 20-week m.a., as at point B, or point C, and take the profit
a year later when it breaks back below the m.a., as at point D.

However, don't be misled. For illustration purposes I chose two
trades on the chart that worked out well. But, note that for instance
in 2004, there were a number of whipsawing trades that would not
have worked out using just a moving average as the signal genera-
tor.

Therefore, few savvy investors would trade or invest using only
a moving average as an indicator of market direction. They would

want their buy and sell signals supported by other technical indicators, as well as seasonality, investor sentiment, indications of insider buying or selling, and the like.

HOW ARE MOVING AVERAGES CALCULATED?

The term 'moving average' refers to the fact that a set of numbers is being averaged as the numbers move through time.

For instance, to begin calculating a 21-day moving average of Microsoft, the closing prices of Microsoft over the last 21 days are added together, then divided by 21. That provides the average price at which Microsoft sold over the last 21 days. That point is marked on the chart today. That point may be above or below Microsoft's closing price today. That is, Microsoft may currently be above or below its 21-day m.a. To make the average move, each subsequent day the same process is repeated, and the new point is added to the chart. After a few weeks you will have the 21-day moving average moving along the chart where its relationship to Microsoft's current price each day can be seen. In calculating the m.a. each day, the oldest of the 21 closing prices is dropped, and the new day's closing price is added. In other words, only the prices over the most recent 21 days are added together and divided by 21 to calculate the position of the m.a. for that day.

Of course to calculate a 20-week moving average you would continuously average the *weekly* closes for the preceding 20 weeks, and so forth.

Fortunately, we no longer have to laboriously plot moving averages manually as we did 'in the old days'. Now, at very low cost, we simply download the daily closes of stocks and market indexes via computer each day. The computer will then calculate any m.a. we might want to use, and draw it on the chart in a split second. Investors can also go to free websites like BigCharts.com, enter the symbol for a stock, mutual fund, or market index, and the moving average they would like to include, and the chart will instantly appear for analysis.

Variations of Moving Averages.

The moving averages shown in the charts so far are known as 'simple' moving averages. Numerous variations have been developed over the years, wherein 'weightings' are applied to the data (market closes) used in the calculations. The theory for some of them is that as a rally or correction moves along, its recent action is more important than the older activity.

However, while weighted moving averages have their champions, there is little evidence that they're worth the extra effort. As in most endeavors, in technical analysis simple is rarely defeated by complexity.

Moving Average Crossover Indicators.

A single moving average provides evidence of whether a trend remains in place. It is only when the stock or index being tracked breaks through the moving average, either to the downside in the case of a rally, or to the upside in the case of a preceding correction, that an investor needs to be concerned that a trend may be reversing.

I say *may* be reversing because the moving average being breached is not an infallible signal that the market's direction has

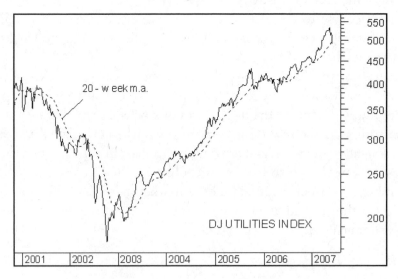

changed. Whipsaws can take place, in which the market crosses and re-crosses the moving average several times before its next direction is revealed. That can be seen in the preceding chart in which a 20-week m.a. is applied to the DJ Utilities Average.

Note how often, especially in early 2001, the index whipsawed up and down across the moving average, in failed signals that were not followed by a sustained trend reversal.

'Moving Average Crossover' indicators were developed to improve on that situation by producing buy and sell signals with fewer whipsaws or failed signals.

The idea is to use two moving averages, one 'faster' than the other.

In the following chart I have applied both a 10-week, and a 30-week moving average to the same chart of the DJ Utilities Average, and placed the moving averages in a separate 'window' of the chart so we can more clearly see when they 'cross'.

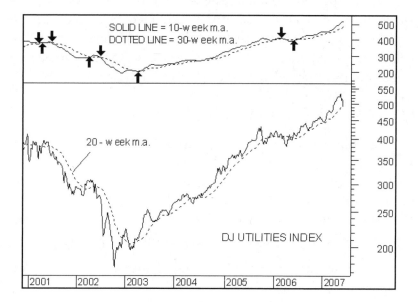

The slower m.a., depicted by the dotted line, is a 30-week m.a. of the Utilities Index, while the faster m.a., depicted by the solid line, is a 10-week m.a. of the index.

When the Utilities Index (lower window of chart) reverses direction, the faster 10-week m.a. reverses faster than the slower 30-week m.a. If the index's change of direction has sufficient staying power, the 10-week m.a. will cross over the slower 30-week m.a. When that happens, a signal is 'triggered'. A buy signal is triggered if the crossover takes place to the upside, and a sell signal if the crossover takes place to the downside.

Note that the use of two moving averages resulted in fewer whipsaws. Only two of the sell signals, and two of the buy signals, that were triggered over the six years were incorrect. The profits on the remaining four signals (buy signals in 2003 and 2006, and sell signals in 2001 and 2002), more than offset the small losses on the failed signals.

Much work on moving-average cross-over systems has taken place over the years, particularly since the introduction of personal computers in the 1980s.

One of the most popular, the Moving-Average Convergence-Divergence (MACD) indicator was developed by Gerald Appel of Signalert Corporation. It uses three different moving averages. We will discuss it in more detail later, as it is an integral component of one of my recommended market-beating strategies.

RELATIVE STRENGTH INDEX (RSI).

The Relative Strength Index, introduced in 1978 by J. Welles Wilder, compares a stock or index's current strength with its *own* strength in the past. It could therefore more accurately be named the *Internal* Strength Index.

RSI is a valuable technical tool, providing several measurements of what can be expected from a stock or index going forward.

1. It identifies the direction of the underlying trend of the stock or index.

2. It measures possible overbought and oversold extremes.

3. It points out divergences, which frequently provide advance notice of a trend reversal.

The following chart of the stock of Best Buy illustrates several ways of utilizing the Relative Strength Index. It is an intermediate-term chart, based on weekly data. We have used a 10-week RSI, shown in the upper window of the chart.

RSI normally tracks between its oversold zone of 30 and its overbought zone of 70. When RSI becomes overbought (at 70 or above), it's usually time to watch for the stock (or a market index) to potentially reverse direction to the downside. When RSI has reached its oversold zone, at 30 or below, it's time to watch for a potential reversal of the stock to the upside.

RSI will also sometimes show a 'divergence' between the internal strength of the stock and the stock's performance. That is, the stock may reach a new rally high, but RSI does not 'confirm' that new high, but instead makes a lower high. That indication of a failure in internal strength is often an indication that the stock's rally has run out of steam and a decline is near. I have marked the above chart with short lines showing when RSI was in divergence (making lower highs while Best Buy was making higher highs).

In the other direction, note how in late 2002, as the stock made successive new lows, RSI was not confirming the new lows (it was making successive *higher* lows). That improvement in the internal strength of the stock even as the stock itself was still hitting new lows, provided advance notice to watch for an *upside* reversal in the stock.

While in this chart it may look like RSI by itself is a foolproof indicator, again I must caution you that there is no such thing as a single perfect indicator that works all the time, or that works with all stocks or markets. Technical analysts will usually apply several different indicators and moving averages to their chart, insisting on having confirming signals from several before making a trade.

TRENDLINES AND TRADING CHANNELS.

Many stocks trade in patterns that make the use of trendlines and trading channels very useful tools in timing the stock or index. The following chart of General Motors is an example.

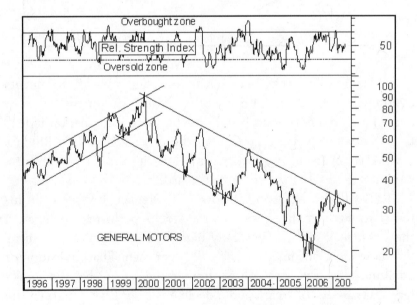

In the 1990's bull market, GM was in a strong long-term up-trend. However within that long-term trend, it still traded in intermediate-term rallies and corrections, confined within a long-term trading band. Each intermediate-term rally was halted by the upper limit of the trading band, while each correction found support at the lower limit of the band. Trading those rallies and corrections, each lasting six months or so, using just the limits of the trading band as signals of when to buy and sell, produced a much larger gain over those four years than simply buying and holding GM. Some of its intermediate-term corrections lasted as long as 10 months, and amounted to 15% or more.

Yet, even a buy and hold investor, not interested in making those intermediate-term trades, would still benefit from watching such a chart. He or she would be less worried by each of those intermediate-term corrections, expecting they would end once GM reached the support at the lower limit of the band.

Likewise, when the bear market struck in 2000, and GM began a multi-year down trend, it was not a straight line down. As with most stocks, GM traded with numerous substantial bear market rallies that lasted for up to a year, and produced gains of 50% or more. Yet each of those rallies and subsequent corrections was confined within a clear trading band, which helped define when the intermediate-term rallies and corrections would end.

Note that the addition of the RSI indicator in the upper window of the chart helped define when GM was overbought or oversold and due for reversals. RSI also identified when GM was overbought in 2001 even though GM itself did not reach the upper limit of its trading band.

This chart is another example of how technical analysis provides its information and signals without being thrown off by what analysis of surrounding conditions might have the crowd expecting at the time.

That's all we're going to talk about chart analysis for now, just enough to have you understand its usefulness in avoiding the thinking of the 'crowd'.

We're going to move on to an understanding of the second of the four legs of technical analysis—investor sentiment.

Chapter 10

Investor Sentiment—Avoiding the Crowd

We've already talked some about the importance of investor sentiment; how the majority, or 'crowd', is usually wrong at important market turning points.

As the stock market cycles back and forth between rallies and corrections, investor confidence cycles back and forth between optimism and pessimism. Unfortunately, investor confidence reaches an extreme of optimism and the strongest urge to buy at exactly the wrong time, near market tops. In the other direction, pessimism and a fear-filled urge to sell reach an extreme after a serious correction has the market oversold, with prices on the bargain table—when it's actually time to buy.

As I noted in an earlier chapter, famed investor (and market-timer) Warren Buffett puts it this way; "What the wise man does at the beginning [of a rising or falling market] the fool does at the end." And in explaining the great track record that made him a multi-billionaire, he says, "I simply attempt to be fearful when others are greedy, and greedy when others are fearful."

Numerous studies have been conducted, and books written on the subject of crowd psychology. *The Crowd—A Study of the Popular Mind*, written in the late 19th century by French Social scientist Gustave LeBon, is one of the best, but is unfortunately out of print.

LeBon had this to say about individuals becoming caught up in the thinking of crowds:

"In its ordinary sense, the word 'crowd' simply means a gathering of individuals of similar interests, nationality, profession, or situation that brings them together in one place. However, from the psychological point of view the expression 'crowd' assumes quite a different significance."

"Under certain circumstances, and only under those circumstances, a crowd of people takes on a character of its own, as a group, which is very different from the characteristics of the individual people composing the group. At such times the sentiments and ideas of all the persons in the gathering take one and the same direction, and their individual conscious personalities vanish. A collective mind is formed presenting very clearly defined characteristics. The gathering has thus become what, in the absence of a better expression, I will call a psychological crowd. It forms a single being, and is subject to the laws of the mental unity of crowds."

"The most striking peculiarity presented by a psychological crowd is the following: Whoever be the individuals that compose it, however like or unlike be their normal mode of life, occupations, individual characters, or their intelligence, the fact that they have been transformed into a psychological crowd puts them in possession of a sort of collective mind. It makes them feel, think, and act in a manner quite different from what each individual would feel, think, and act were he in a state of mental isolation from the others."

"It is only by obtaining some sort of insight into the psychology of crowds that it can be understood how powerless the individuals within the crowd are to hold opinions other than those which are imposed upon them as a group. It is not with rules based on rational thinking that they are led, but by whatever produces a superficial impression on them, and what seduces them."

Examples of how individuals who are caught up in the 'mental unity' of a crowd, think and act differently than they do as individuals can be seen when 'nice' teen-agers get caught up in 'crowd thinking' at parties that get out of control, in shopper riots by normally calm ladies at openings for widely advertised store sales, in contagious responses at religious revivals, and so on.

Analysts of crowd behavior are particularly fascinated by the way crowd psychology takes over people with similar interests even though the participants are not gathered in one place. The participants are described as a 'diffused crowd'.

LeBon found that the formation of 'diffused crowds' usually results from large amounts of one-sided information being disseminated over a broad area. It might be through advertising, publicity, government propaganda, or repetitive news items distributed by the mass media. LeBon said that the key is that little or no opposing information is provided to create a balance.

On a grand scale, LeBon referred to how Napoleon's grasp of crowd psychology enabled him to convince France of its invincibility, that it could conquer the world. Adolph Hitler, and the leaders of various revolutions, similarly understood crowd psychology, and manipulated it to achieve their goals.

But, how do investors periodically get caught up in the 'mental unity' of a psychological crowd?

Psychologists define three fundamental human emotions; joy, fear, and anger. The first two manifest themselves in crowd psychology extremes as; joyful euphoria, as in a strong bull market when big profits are being made effortlessly; and panic (fear), as in a stock market crash or bear market when large losses are being experienced. The third emotion, anger, takes over a crowd for example at a store opening for a special sale when a few aggressive individuals try to push to the front of the line.

Keep in mind that according to LeBon the key is "little to no opposing information being provided that would create a balance."

After a bull market has been running awhile the profits become exciting for those who have been participating, and the word begins to spread. However, there is still plenty of skepticism and concern around. Every once in awhile the market experiences a brief setback that reminds investors that investing is not free of risk. Opposing opinions are plentiful, and investors must make up their minds individually.

However, as the bull market continues, the market's brief setbacks repeatedly prove to be buying opportunities rather than the beginning of serious problems. The skepticism diminishes. Opposing opinions begin to disappear. The profits continue to grow. It becomes great fun for more and more people to constantly check the market to see how much money is being made. It's so enjoyable to talk with friends and associates about the profits, and pass along tips about stocks, tips that almost always work out.

The joy and optimism spread and those emotions take over an increasingly larger majority of investors. Wall Street, always 90% bullish in its outlook, stokes the fire. Those urging caution are increasingly brushed aside as not understanding, and tired of being ridiculed recede into the background. The information investors are receiving becomes increasingly one-sided. The psychology of a diffused crowd is taking over. The mass media gets caught up in the excitement and is soon feeding the frenzy, passing along the bullish and positive opinions of the majority, with little in the way of opposing opinions or information for investors to consider.

Yet we know the market does not move in endless trends. We have seen the proof in 200 years of the U.S. market's activity, and for many centuries in the markets of Europe.

Eventually the price of every investment, be it real estate, art, beanie babies, or stocks, will become too extreme, too overvalued. Smart money begins to take their profits and the top is in. And since investor excitement and confidence has continued to grow with the rising prices, it is inevitable that the 'crowd' will be at an extreme of optimism when a market reaches its top. It cannot be otherwise.

However, comes the inevitable swing of the pendulum in the other direction, the bear market that follows every bull market, and investor psychology begins to change.

Prices begin to decline. The first stage for the 'psychological crowd' is denial that the bull market has ended. The crowd continues to buy the dips in prices, convinced they are still buying opportunities. But as each dip is followed by a brief rally attempt that fails, with the downside resuming, optimism turns to concern. As previous market gains begin to disappear, concern turns to worry. As losses become larger and more painful, worry turns to fear, and eventually panic.

The stock market has become a painful subject. The previous enjoyment of discussing stocks and the market with friends is replaced by embarrassment to even admit being involved in it. Even Wall Street has stopped talking about the market decline being a temporary setback, and begins talking about what it might take to eventually get conditions turned around.

Fear and pessimism take over the thinking of the majority. The psychological crowd has formed, now bearish and pessimistic. And the collective mind has closed. Surrounding conditions are terrible. Bad news is so dominating everything they hear and read, that the majority of investors want nothing to do with thoughts that it might be time to begin buying again.

Only after the next bull market has been underway long enough to again create optimism and excitement in the media does their courage return.

Obviously, as Warren Buffett and all successful investors point out, **avoidance of crowd thinking is extremely important to investing success.**

In their efforts to avoid getting caught up in crowd psychology, professionals and serious investors therefore watch investor sentiment closely.

ONLY EXTREMES ARE OF IMPORTANCE.

It's important to realize that the bullishness or bearishness of investors is meaningless most of the time. It is only when bullishness reaches an extreme (near market tops), or bearishness reaches an extreme (near market bottoms), that investor sentiment begins to have meaning.

It is also important to realize that an indication of extreme bullishness or bearishness is not a buy or sell 'signal'. Sentiment can remain at extreme readings for quite some time before market reversals actually take place.

Excessive crowd bullishness can therefore only be used as a measurement of risk, telling market technicians when to more closely watch their charts for overbought conditions, when to be ready to take their profits if important support levels, such as moving averages, are broken.

In the other direction, extremes of bearish investor sentiment can only be used as an early indication that a market decline may soon reach a bottom.

Not all groups represent the usually wrong 'crowd'.

Years of statistics have shown a strong tendency for certain groups of investors to form the usually wrong psychological crowd at market turning points. Other groups tend to have the ability to avoid 'crowd think', and are usually right at the turning points.

So in technical analysis the idea is to compare the sentiment of those groups that are usually right, to the sentiment of those groups that constitute the 'crowd' that is usually wrong at turning points.

Those who, *as a group*, tend to be wrong at market turning points include:

1. The media (print and TV)

2. Public investors

3. Futures traders

4. Options traders

5. Newsletter writers

Don't misunderstand. Many individuals among them will be right (by not being part of their crowd) at market turning points. However, the majority of each group, therefore the group when measured as a whole, tends to be bullish and confident at market tops, and bearish and fearful near important market lows.

Their sentiment is known as a 'contrary indicator', since when it reaches extremes of either bullishness or bearishness, the market almost always soon moves contrary to that opinion.

Those who, *as a group*, tend to be right at market turning points include;

1. Wall Street professionals

2. Financial institutions

3. Corporate insiders

4. NYSE members.

Here again, some among them will be wrong, but as a group, they tend not to get caught up in the crowd's emotions of euphoria or fear.

They tend to sell into the strength as a stock, or the market nears a top, taking and keeping their profits rather than giving them back in the next market decline.

In the other direction, they ignore the extreme gloom of the crowd psychology that is present at important market lows, recognizing before others that economic changes are underway that will not be obvious to outsiders for some time. They begin the buying that launches the next bull market.

Can 'smart money' be depended on to inform others when they are buying or selling?

No. In fact, what they say publicly is often just the opposite of what they are actually doing. Keep in mind that they are on the playing field to score their own profits. So they tend to use their influence, particularly with the media, to fool the other players into helping them score. Thus during a bull market, when they are loaded up with stocks and want the market to move higher, they make the rounds of financial shows promoting bullishness to drive prices higher. Everyone benefits from their advice as the market moves higher.

However, when the market eventually becomes overbought (keep in mind that a bear market arrives on average of every four years) they begin selling to take profits. Yet they often continue to appear on the financial show circuit touting the market as being in good shape and encouraging others to 'buy the dips'. That of course creates additional strength into which they can continue to sell at high prices.

When they have completed their selling they have no reason to want the market to continue rising. In fact, they want the market to decline so they can load up on stocks at the next bottom at lower prices. At that point they become less bullish in their interviews, speaking more of the risk of still lower prices. Public investors finally realize the market is in a correction, that 'dips' are not buying opportunities. They begin selling and the market declines more seriously. Near the correction's bottom, when the 'smart money' wants to load up again at the low prices, they remain bearish in their interviews, warning that the decline might have further to go.

In a surprisingly candid interview in December, 2006, former hedge-fund manager James Cramer, now a well-known TV financial show host, admitted as much, saying. *"What's important when you are in that hedge-fund mode is to not say anything remotely truthful, because the truth is so against your goals. It's important to create a new truth, to develop a fiction,"*

The investigations after the 2000-2002 bear market revealed how in the previous bull market, near its top in 1999, brokerage firm analysts produced glowing reports on companies for public consumption, while calling the companies "dogs" and worse in their private e-mails among each other. And corporate insiders were selling their stocks heavily, while appearing on TV financial shows telling the public how great the future looked for their companies.

Since they do not get caught up in the 'psychological crowd' thinking at the market's turning points, is the 'smart money' more intelligent than those who do get caught up in the crowd?

Certainly not! The popularized term 'smart money' is a misnomer. I find it offensive, as should most investors. A more accurate term would be 'insiders'. But that may be taken incorrectly, as meaning only corporate insiders, whereas the 'smart money' is considered to be those who professionally manage very large amounts of money; pension plans, insurance companies, investment banks, trust companies, and very large private investors.

The only element that makes them seem smarter is their professional positions. They have more facts, data, and inside contacts than any outsider, particularly individual investors, could hope to have. They are therefore in a position to make their decisions based on facts rather than emotions. Thus is the playing field so significantly tilted in their favor.

It can also be said that to no small degree, through their public appearances and pronouncements, they are also the fuel that drives public investors into a 'psychological crowd' mindset of extreme euphoria at market tops, and extreme pessimism at market bottoms. So they are not likely to fall for their own hype.

MEASURING SENTIMENT.

The Media.

I listed the print and TV media first among those who develop into a 'psychological crowd' as market turning points approach for a reason. They not only become a psychological crowd themselves, but have the most responsibility, right up there with Wall Street, for turning public investors into a psychological crowd at exactly the wrong times in the cycles.

They can't help themselves. They are reporters of economic and investment news and opinions. Just as sportswriters, journalists covering show business, politics, or any specialized area, must depend on their sources within the specific industry for information and opinions, so must those covering the economic and investing scene. That means the financial media must depend on Wall Street firms for interviews and opinions (while the media owners depend on the same firms for their advertising revenue).

Therefore, as I earlier quoted $140 billion dollar money-manager Jeremy Grantham as saying, *"Investors need to be aware that everything they hear or read is always 90% dripping in bullish bias. It sells stocks, and for the record it sells books and magazines."*

It cannot be otherwise then that the media is at the top of the list as being in the usually wrong 'psychological crowd' at important market turning points.

It's difficult to measure when media sentiment has taken on the characteristics of a psychological crowd. They don't conduct polls of themselves. They don't tell stories on themselves of how incorrectly optimistic they were at previous market tops, or how bearish they were at previous market bottoms.

The only information regarding the media's role at market tops and bottoms comes from independent financial newsletters. They are not exactly scientific measurements, but are interesting.

As far back as the 1970s, newsletters were compiling what they called magazine cover 'indicators'. They work like this:

A new bull market gets underway when insiders and 'smart money' professionals and institutions believe a bear market has ended and they begin buying. The next in line of those beginning to believe will be knowledgeable and experienced public investors, especially if they are watching charts and see that money has begun flowing into the market again. They will eventually be followed by not-so-experienced investors when they finally see a bull market has clearly been underway for awhile and become fearful of being left behind. If the bull market lasts long enough, people who do not normally invest in the stock market will hear of the money their neighbors and friends are making in the market, and will become new investors.

By the time that interest in the market, and knowledge of how well it has been doing, becomes so widely recognized that main-stream—non-financial—magazines (Newsweek, Time, etc.) are publishing bullish 'cover' stories on it, it is thought that the end is near.

In the opposite direction, by the time the misery caused by a bear market has reached the point of being reported in 'cover' stories in non-financial magazines, the bear market is usually just about over.

As an example, *Schaeffer's Investment Research* tracked when 'mainstream' non-financial magazines finally became interested enough in the stock market to feature it on their covers. The firm found 38 times over the years when the cover stories were bullish. On average the stock market was *down* 7% three months after the cover appeared. It found 12 times when the cover stories were bearish. Two months later the market was 7% higher.

However, investor sentiment is most often measured by means of scientific polls of specific groups of market participants.

The *American Association of Individual Investors* (AAII), based in Chicago, collects data weekly from a sampling of its members, and reports the percentage that are bullish, bearish, or neutral on the market.

The poll has a history of showing that when individual investors as a group are more than 50% bullish while fewer than 25% are bearish (the rest being neutral), the market is in danger of a correction, while when more than 50% are bearish and fewer than 25% are bullish, a market rally soon begins.

Since the mood of individual investors tends to swing back and forth quickly, becoming more bullish with each small rally of a few weeks duration, and more bearish after a market pullback of only a few weeks duration, the AAII sentiment readings are utilized more as a short-term trading tool.

Consensus Inc., Kansas City, Missouri, polls and reports the sentiment of professional brokers and money-managers.

Market Vane, Pasadena, California, reports the bullish, bearish, and neutral percentages of futures traders.

The *Commodity Futures Trading Commission (CFTC)* also measures the sentiment of futures traders. The CFTC requires futures traders to report their trades in a timely manner. It then breaks that activity down to provide a weekly *'Commitment of Traders Report'*, which compares the trading activity of various types of market traders (professionals, speculators, commercial hedgers, and small traders). The ratios of the long, or short-sale, positions of each group are used to compare their relative bullish or bearish sentiment.

The *Chicago Board Options Exchange* (CBOT) provides its *VIX Volatility Index*, sometimes referred to as the "Investor Fear Index".

It measures the volatility in the premiums that options traders are willing to pay for options on the S&P 500 Index.

When the VIX Index reaches high readings it signifies options traders have become fearful and pessimistic to an extreme, perhaps indicating the market is oversold and a rally is likely to begin. When the VIX Index reaches extreme low readings, it is a warning that options traders may have been made too optimistic by a rising market, that the market may be overbought and due for a decline.

The following chart illustrates its use.

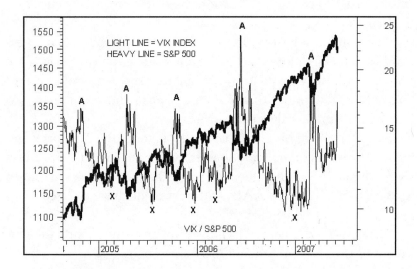

I have placed an X on the VIX Index when it was at low readings indicating a high level of investor optimism and bullishness. That is when the S&P 500 is at risk of topping out. Conversely, the VIX Index tends to be at high readings, which I have marked A, indicating a high level of investor pessimism, when market corrections end.

Then there are *Put/Call Ratios*. Investors buy Put Options when they expect a stock, sector, or market to decline, and Call Options when rising prices are expected. So Put/Call ratios, comparing the demand for Put Options to the demand for Call Options, also indicate whether options players as a group are optimistic or pessimistic about the market's prospects.

Investors Intelligence, founded in 1947 by the legendary A.W. Cohen, but now a subsidiary of Stockcube plc, a United Kingdom company, tracks the sentiment of investment advisory newsletters, releasing its findings weekly to its subscribers. The majority of newsletters are invariably very bullish at market tops and very bearish at market lows. That statistic has led to the popular conception that newsletter sentiment is also a contrary indicator.

However, while it is true that the majority of newsletters are bullish at market tops and bearish at market lows, the statistic is a bit misleading. Often the majority has been bullish throughout a bull market, and although still bullish at market tops, quickly become bearish and remain bearish all the way down in a bear market. So, because the majority of newsletters have reached an extreme of bullishness does not necessarily mean the market is near a top. As noted, they can reach that extreme early in a bull market and remain very bullish all the way to its top.

Because of that history of the newsletter 'crowd' often being right, we have newsletter sentiment at the bottom of our list of the usually wrong 'crowds'.

Tracking the sentiment of the usually right groups.

Corporate insiders must report their buying and selling activity to the Securities & Exchange Commission (SEC) in a timely manner, usually within two or three days of the trade. Their activity provides a measurement of their bullish or bearish sentiment for their own company, or cumulatively for specific sectors, and the overall market.

The raw data on insider buying and selling is available to all investors at the SEC's website (www.SEC.gov). However, the raw data is voluminous and confusing. There are roughly 2,000 filings *per day*, the majority of which are unimportant. Therefore, a number of research sources compile the data into useful formats and make it available to investors, usually by subscription. The largest and best known is Thompson Financial (www.thompson.com).

Others include www.insidertoday.com, and www.insider-transactions.com.

Tracking the activity and sentiment of *NYSE members* is a bit more difficult, and less precise. Every week, the NYSE issues reports on the activity of its members, including its floor traders and 'specialists'. (NYSE specialists are those member firms assigned to a 'specialist post' where they each control the trading in a number of listed stocks). The NYSE releases its member trading information on Fridays, but with a two week delay. The report includes the number and volume of stock purchases and sales made by members, including Specialists and Floor Traders, as well as the volume of short-sales by both NYSE members and public investors. The ratio of short-selling by members, compared to short-selling by public investors, is used as a guide to which group is either more (or less) bullish.

- Crowd psychology and investor sentiment is a large topic, but all we need to know for our purposes is that when the sentiment of the 'psychological crowd' reaches an extreme of optimism and bullishness it's time to be watching for a potentially important market top, and when it reaches an extreme of pessimism and bearishness it's time to be watching for a potentially important correction bottom and buying opportunity.

Now at last.

You have enough basic information about how the markets work, and the forces that are lined up against you in the game.

It's time to move on to the most important tool in market-timing, and a great friend to public investors—the market's seasonality.

PART 2

Now You Are Ready!

INTRODUCING THE SEASONAL STRATEGIES!

Chapter 11

The Market's Amazing Seasonal Patterns

I can give only general credit to those who pioneered discoveries regarding the market's seasonal patterns. The exact provenance of some has become clouded as they passed from hand to hand and into the public domain, including, as Robert Prechter of Elliott Wave fame claims, instances of 'intellectual piracy'.

Arthur Merrill was an early pioneer in researching market patterns, compiling them in his now rare and out-of-print 1965 book *Behavior of Prices on Wall Street.*

Market historian Yale Hirsch began publishing *The Stock Traders Almanac* in 1968. It contained historical market statistics and patterns known at the time, and has been updated annually since. (The Almanac was sold to book publisher John Wiley & Sons in 2005).

Norman Fosback teamed up with Glen King Parker to found *The Institute for Econometric Research* in 1971. Its goal was to conduct scientific research into the behavior of stock prices. The Institute compiled a large computerized database of market statistics and research of the previous century. It used that database to develop mathematical forecasting techniques, creating, testing, and developing concepts and models to predict market performance.

In 1976, Fosback published *Market Logic*, a compilation of previous research and studies, some of which began back in the 1800s, along with new information developed by his Institute for Econometric Research.

Over the following 28 years The Institute for Econometric Research launched nine newsletters, by which it passed its recommendations along to public and professional investors. One of those newsletters was *The Insiders*, a popular source of information on the buying and selling activity of corporate insiders. With impressive timing, Fosback sold The Institute for Econometric Research to *Time Inc.* in 1999. That was just before the devastating 2000-2002 bear market wiped out many investors, which resulted in a drastic decline in the subscriber base of investment newsletters. Time Inc. ceased publication of the newsletters a year later.

Ned Davis founded the still highly regarded *Ned Davis Research Inc.* in 1980. Over the years, Davis's research has included numerous important studies regarding the market's seasonal patterns. His firm's research is available primarily to large institutions.

My own Asset Management Research Corp., founded in 1988, has added important new information on the market's seasonal patterns over the last 20 years. It provides the information to investors in a newsletter, *Sy Harding's Street Smart Report*, and on the Internet via Street Smart Report Online (www.streetsmartreport.com). Its subscribers are approximately 50% institutions and money-management firms, and 50% public investors.

Most previous research, including my own, had resulted in generalized commentaries about the market's seasonality, as interesting observations more than anything else.

However, for my 1999 book *Riding the Bear—How to Prosper in the Coming Bear Market*, I was searching for a specific strategy that would work in both bull and bear markets, and would protect investors in the serious bear market that I expected.

After much research the market's seasonal tendencies stood out as having the best potential for providing such a strategy. After still further research, back-testing and work we developed a strategy that harnesses the proven consistency of the market's annual seasonal patterns. Back-tested over the previous 50 years in the research, the strategy more than doubled the performance of the S&P 500 over the long term. Used in real time in the Street Smart Report newsletter it has continued that performance, more than doubling the performance of the S&P 500 over the last nine years.

Further, it had no losing years, even though the severe 2000-2002 bear market took place during the period.

So, a large body of work has shown that the stock market moves in very consistent short-term, intermediate-term, and long-term patterns. **Being aware of, and understanding those patterns, can make a dramatic difference in the profits of investors.**

INTRADAY MARKET PATTERNS.

Intraday and short-term patterns are used primarily by short-term traders. *However, awareness of even those patterns can add to profits for longer-term investors who keep them in mind when placing their buy and sell orders.*

Studies of the market's movements during a typical trading day show that while it opens in one direction or the other, that direction often lasts for only an hour or two. The initial move usually reverses direction for the middle hours of the day. It is then the final hour or two that determines whether the market will be up or down at the end of the trading day.

It is thought the first hour or two of trading is dominated by overnight orders placed by individual investors via their personal computers when the markets are closed, while institutional investors and professional traders take over after the markets have been open awhile.

The theory is that public investors get home from work after the market has closed each day. Only then do many find out how the market closed. If they have an investment decision to make they look through financial publications in the evening, and perhaps surf the Internet looking for more information.

Many will then place their order to buy or sell via their PC, even though the market is closed. Others may postpone their final decision until the next morning, in order to catch the overnight news and the economic reports that are released early the following morning. But then they also tend to enter their orders with their brokerage firm via their PC before the market opens, so they can get off to work on time, or in the case of retirees, off to their golf game.

There is a limited after-hours marketplace where orders for *some* individual stocks can be executed when the market is closed (via 'Electronic Communications Networks, or ECNs), if an investor has that type of account. But the stocks available for trading on ECNs is very limited, and mutual funds and exchange-traded-funds are not included at all. Dominated by institutions, it is also a very risky environment for individual investors.

Most orders placed by investors via their PCs when the market is closed are placed in their normal online brokerage accounts to be executed when the market opens. They are placed after-hours only because the investors will be otherwise occupied when the market is open.

Those orders then accumulate, waiting to be matched by the specialists and market-makers at the open. Those placed as 'limit' orders, meaning they cannot be executed unless and until the stock trades at a specified price, may not be executed until the market has been open awhile (and perhaps not at all if market-moving news has come out when the market was closed).

Due to the heavy back-up of overnight orders the market's initial move after it opens is often overdone in one direction or the other. Professional traders therefore tend to wait until that initial move has run its course, then take positions for a quick trade in the opposite direction. So a market that might have begun the day to the downside will almost always run into a 'countertrend' rally for several hours, even if it resumes its original direction a few hours later. A market that begins the day to the upside will almost always pull back to lower levels for awhile mid-day.

However, the market's action in the final hour of the day is looked on as the most important indication of the market's true trend, since it is thought to be dominated by professional and institutional investors. They watch the market's action through the day, analyze the latest economic news, and make their trades while the market is still open (when they can know the prices at which the trades will be executed).

An old Wall Street maxim says that "A market that is weak in the morning but strong in the afternoon is in bull market mode, while a market that is strong in the morning but weak in the afternoon is in bear market mode."

That reflects Wall Street's thinking that public investors dominate what happens in the morning, while the expectations of 'smart money' dominates in the afternoon, especially in the final hour, and is more likely to be right.

UTILIZING THE COUNTER-TREND MOVE.

The odds of a counter-trend move taking place after the market has been open for an hour or two is consistent enough that we advise investors to avoid reacting in panic to an opening move if it is opposite to what they need to get a timely price. If they wait an hour or two the market will likely change direction, at least for awhile.

We also advise investors *not* to place buy or sell orders in the evening, since news or events that take place prior to the open in the morning can have a dramatic effect on opening prices the next day. That is particularly true now that the world has become so much a worldwide economy. Whatever happens in the day-time hours in foreign countries (nighttime hours in the U.S.), can have a significant effect on the way the U.S. market opens the following day. It is therefore much wiser to make trades when the market is open, when current bid and asked prices are available.

However, the intraday market pattern is of limited value except to day-traders.

Let's move on now to specific investing strategies that harness seasonal patterns to outperform the market.

Chapter 12

The *Monthly* Seasonal Timing Strategy

MONTHLY SEASONAL PATTERNS.

It's no secret that when a larger than normal amount of money chases after a product in any market, be it stocks, real estate, or Beanie Babies, the price is going to rise.

A seasonal pattern based on just such a flow of extra money into the stock market on certain days of the month provides the basis of an exceptional seasonal investment strategy.

Norman Fosback's *Institute for Econometric Research* discovered back in the 1970s that the stock market tends to concentrate most of its gains each month in just the last trading day of the month, and the first four trading days of the following month. He published that information in his 1976 book, *Stock Market Logic*.

In more recent years, Fosback refined the pattern to include the last *two* days of each month, and the first *five* trading days of the following month, plus the two days in advance of holidays on which the New York Stock Exchange will be closed.

Where does that money come from, and why is it concentrated in just a few days surrounding the end of each month?

A lot of it comes from dividends and interest payments. In 1990 *The Journal of Finance* published a study by Professor Joseph P. Ogden of the State University of New York. It showed that 45% of all common stock dividends, 65% of all preferred stock dividends, and 90% of interest payments on municipal bonds, is paid to investors on either the first or last day of each month. It amounts to tens of billions of dollars. Most investors designate that their investment accounts provide automatic re-investment of those dividends.

Still more money flows in at the end of each month from investors following the popular strategy of dollar-cost averaging into the market on a monthly basis.

Substantial amounts flow in at month-end from automatic monthly contributions by employers and employees to their 401K and IRA plans.

Many mutual funds and money-management firms collect their management fees on a monthly basis, and invest those fees in the market when received.

Many high-income employees receive their salaries monthly rather than weekly.

Most commission salesmen, real estate brokers, and stock-brokers, receive their commissions and bonuses on a monthly basis.

In total it amounts to tens of billions, if not hundreds of billions, of extra money flowing into the market on the days surrounding the end of the month, frequently producing larger than normal stock gains on those days. Studies have shown that on average the market makes close to half of its gains for the month during those seven trading days.

It is not quite as easy to explain why the market tends to make larger than normal gains for the two days prior to holidays.

The most logical explanation is that U.S. short-sellers do not like to be holding short-sale positions when the U.S. market is closed, especially if foreign markets are open. The risk is that something may happen over the long weekend, or in international markets on the holiday, that will cause the U.S. market to open sharply higher the day after the holiday, handing them large losses. Therefore many short-sellers move to the buy side to close out those short-sale positions in advance of three-day holiday weekends, producing a so-called 'short-covering rally' over the two trading days prior to the holiday.

In any event, regardless of the reasons, it has been happening for at least 80 years.

HARNESSING THE PATTERN AS A STRATEGY.

The rules:

- Enter the market for the seven days consisting of the last two trading days of each month, and the first five trading days of the following month. Then exit to collect interest on cash for the rest of the month.

- Enter the market again for the two days prior to holidays, *if the NYSE will be closed.* Then exit to collect interest on cash.

Sound Mind Investing published a report based on Fosback's back-testing of that strategy for the period of 1927—1990.

The report assumes two portfolios, each started with $10,000.

One portfolio owns the stocks of the DJIA only for the 'favorable' days each month, and is in cash the rest of the time. The other portfolio takes the opposite approach. It remains in cash during the 'favorable' days, and invests only for the 'unfavorable' days each month.

By 1990, the portfolio invested only during the 'favorable' days had grown to $4,400,000. The other portfolio, although in the market more than twice as many days each month, saw its value *decline* 95% over the years, winding up at just $433.

Yes, the results for both portfolios in real life would be affected by transaction costs and taxes on short-term capital gains. But the study does clearly show the long-term consistency of the market's monthly seasonal pattern.

In a similar study, Mark Hulbert, editor of the well-known *Hulbert Financial Digest*, measured the performance of the strategy by tracking Norman Fosback's Seasonality Trading System from September, 1985 to September, 2005.

Rather than comparing the performance of the 'favorable' days to the 'unfavorable' days, Hulbert compared the Seasonality Trading System to buy and hold, using $100,000 in the Dow Jones Wilshire 5000 as the beginning balance in each case.

The following table shows the results.

Dollar Value of Portfolio		
Date	**Wilshire 5000**	**Fosback's Seasonality System**
Sept/1985	$100,000	$100,000
Sept/1986	$130,382	$105,828
Sept/1987	$180,182	$142,731
Sept/1988	$159,819	$178,326
Sept/1989	$209,987	$217,226
Sept/1990	$182,252	$251,952
Sept/1991	$244,655	$307,977
Sept/1992	$270,130	$329,158
Sept/1993	$316,734	$337,763
Sept/1994	$324,789	$352,030
Sept/1995	$419,315	$395,341
Sept/1996	$498,655	$457,293
Sept/1997	$688,288	$566,440
Sept/1998	$710,922	$621,442
Sept/1999	$902,424	$723,875
Sept/2000	$1,060,776	$917,528
Sept/2001	$753,361	$918,975
Sept/2002	$621,358	$893,449
Sept/2003	$776,306	$973,796
Sept/2004	$900,251	$1,076,833
Sept/2005	$1,033,489	$1,256,830
Source: Hulbert Financial Digest.		

OBSERVATIONS:

No strategy works all the time. *It is extremely important to realize that.* Otherwise, you will tend to jump to a different one the first time a proven long-term strategy seems to have failed you.

So note from the table how neither the buy and hold strategy, nor the monthly seasonal strategy, worked in every market period.

Had you started this strategy in 1985, even though making gains for the first two years, you would have been under-performing the market for those two years. You would not have pulled ahead of buy and hold until the third year. You would then have remained ahead of the buy and hold investor for the next seven years. However, when 1995 arrived, although the seasonal strategy continued to make gains for each of the next four years, those gains were not as large as were being made by the buy and hold investor. That's understandable since from 1995 through 1999 the market was in a highly unusual, one-sided, super bull market. But then from 2000 through 2005, you would have continued to make gains, while the market and a buy and hold investor actually had substantial losses.

Therefore, over the long-term you would have out-performed the market in only ten of the twenty years. But because you were in the market on days when the odds were high that it would make gains, and out the rest of the time, large losses were avoided. And so you obtained the superior results of gaining 20% more than the market over the 20-year period.

Of those results Mark Hulbert has this to say: "Over the twenty years, the seasonal strategy portfolio produced a 13.4% annualized total return, in contrast to the Wilshire 5000's 12.0% average annual return. But what makes this timing system's performance so impressive is not that it beat the market. It's that it did so with far less than normal market risk, since it had an investor in the market less than 50% of the time. That is why, *on a risk-adjusted basis*, it is the best-performing market-timing system of any I have tracked at the Hulbert Financial Digest."

There is another important piece of information regarding risk revealed by the performance numbers. Note that the market lost money in four of the twenty 12-month periods. The losses were 11.3%, 13.2%, 30%, and 17.5%. *In only one of the twenty periods did the seasonal strategy have a loss, and that loss was only 2.8%.*

Therefore an investor would have had a much less stressful time following the seasonal strategy, and would have been much more likely to stick with it over the long-term, rather than selling at one of the lows.

This monthly seasonal pattern is also of value to those following other strategies, even a buy and hold strategy.

- Realizing the higher odds of the market being up on particular days of the month, and buying in advance of those days, or waiting to sell until after those days, can add several percentage points annually to the profit on holdings bought in accordance with any strategy.

- An investor who dollar-cost averages into the market on a monthly basis would do well to make those monthly additions a few days before the end of the month to take advantage of the odds of the market being up for those days.

- A retiree taking a fixed amount out of his portfolio each month for living expenses would do himself a favor by doing so after the fifth trading day of the month, rather than at month end.

WILL THE PATTERN CONTINUE?

But you say, as soon as everyone knows about the pattern, too many will begin trading in advance of it in an effort to beat everyone else to the punch, and the pattern will go away.

I seriously doubt that will happen.

To begin with, few investors will ever be aware of it.

Consider that there are more than 40 million investors in the U.S. Yet, even *The Wall Street Journal*, the most read financial publication in the country, has fewer than three million subscribers. And most of those are probably brokers, money-managers, analysts, bankers, and corporate executives. Consider that there are only 400,000 viewers watching CNBC-TV, by far the largest of the financial-TV networks.

So even if the financial media were to report on the validity of the monthly seasonal pattern, rather than following Wall Street's lead of down-playing all seasonal patterns, there will never be more than a very small percentage of investors aware of the pattern. Even fewer would remember to incorporate the pattern when they are making changes in their holdings.

Meanwhile, the flow of additional huge chunks of money into the market at month-end will not change as long as the majority of dividend and interest payments are made at the end of each month; as long as companies and employees make their monthly contributions to 401K and IRA plans at the end of the month; as long as investors engage in dollar-cost-averaging into the market at the end of each month; as long as money-managers and institutions collect their management fees at month end; as long as most executives are paid by the month; as long as salesmen and brokers receive their commissions and bonuses at the end of each month, as long as . . . well you get the picture.

The strategy even eliminates a good portion of market risk.

Keep in mind the three risks in investing in the stock market that we discussed in earlier chapters; market risk, sector risk, and stock risk. We spoke of how we can eliminate stock risk and sector risk (two-thirds of the investing risk) by only buying the market itself, using DJIA or S&P 500 index mutual funds, or index Exchange-Traded-Funds (ETFs).

This seasonal strategy eliminates even a good portion of the remaining risk, market risk, by being in the market less than 50% of the time, and further by being in the market only for the 50% of the time that the market is most likely to make gains, and out of the market when it is most likely to have losses.

And yet the strategy has a history of not just matching the performance of the benchmark S&P 500, but of out-performing it by approximately 20% over the long-term.

THE STRATEGY'S DRAWBACKS.

The Monthly Seasonal Strategy does have a couple of disadvantages.

It involves approximately 20 round trips in and out of the market per year, with holding periods of only a few days each time. In the last few years virtually all no-load index mutual funds have imposed minimum holding periods of 30-days to 6 months on investors. Their early withdrawal fees are as much as 2%. Such a fund would not be usable for the short-term trading required by the monthly seasonal pattern.

Investors can follow the strategy by utilizing index exchange-traded-funds (ETFs), which trade through brokerage firms like stocks and have no minimum holding periods. However, there are broker commissions on each transaction, which although minimal at deep discount brokerage firms, would still cut into profits in a strategy that makes numerous trades, each of which is expected to make only small gains.

So, let's look at another seasonal strategy that delivers even better performance, while also cutting market risk in half, and only requires one round trip trade into and out of the market per year. It can be followed by using no-load index mutual funds or index ETFs.

Chapter 13

The Street Smart Report (Annual) Seasonal Timing Strategy!

Let's begin with some of the previously known annual seasonal patterns.

SELL IN MAY AND GO AWAY.

It has long been realized that the fall and winter months are usually much more positive for the stock market than the summer months.

Ned Davis Research Inc., and Yale Hirsch of the Hirsch Organization, produced numerous studies of the phenomenon over the years. Hirsch published research revealing that the three-month period of August, September, and October, were historically the weakest months of the year for the stock market, while November, December, and January were historically the most positive months.

Ned Davis Research Inc. published numerous studies showing the positive historical results of being invested in the market for the seven month period of October 1 to May 1, and being in cash the other five months.

Hirsch had a different idea about the market's favorable period, calling it a six-month favorable period rather than seven months. He produced studies showing that since 1950 if an investor entered the market on November 1 each year and exited to cash on May 1, remaining in cash for six months each year he (or she) would have just about matched the performance of the S&P 500 over the period. That may not sound exciting. But it is significant. As the numerous studies mentioned earlier show, the great majority of mutual funds and money-managers *fail* to match the performance of the S&P 500, even though working hard at it, and being fully invested all the time. And here is this simple little strategy of buying an index fund on November 1 and selling it on May 1 that not only matches the S&P 500 over the long-term, but does so with only 50% of market risk (since it is safely in cash for six months each year).

While the Davis and Hirsch research disagreed on the best entry date, both found that on average the market's favorable season ended April 31, which contributed to the well-known Wall Street maxim "Sell in May and Go Away".

Alan Newman, editor of the *Crosscurrents* newsletter, back-tested the performance of the Hirsch research from 1950 through April 1997. That was half a century that included all kinds of background conditions, including war and peace, boom times and recessions, bull markets and bear markets.

His study included two portfolios. I will call one the green portfolio and the other the red portfolio. Both began in 1950 with a beginning balance of $100,000. The green portfolio adopted the seasonal strategy of buying the thirty stocks of the DJIA every November 1, selling them April 30, and holding cash until the following November 1.

The red portfolio adopted the opposite strategy. It bought the DJIA on May 1 and sold it on November 1. It was therefore fully invested during the market's unfavorable season, and on the sidelines in cash during the favorable season.

It was no contest. The green portfolio turned the $100,000 into $2,761,113 by May 1, 1997. The red portfolio turned its $100,000 into just $114,840.

That is clear testament to the consistent pattern of favorable and unfavorable annual investment 'seasons'. It prompted Newman to define the period between May 1 and November 1 as the market's 'Dead Season'.

The Davis, Hirsch, and Newman studies did not include the dividends an investor would have received while in the market, nor the interest on cash that a seasonal investor would have received when out of the market.

In some years interest rates on cash have been in double-digits. And over the long-term dividends have accounted for almost half of the stock market's total return.

In 1998, my firm, Asset Management Research Corp., conducted more detailed research to include the effect of dividends and interest on cash. As would be expected, it showed considerably higher total performance for both buy and hold investors, and seasonal investors, during the 50-year period.

But it also confirmed the Ned Davis, Yale Hirsch, and Alan Newman findings that on average almost all of the gains of the market are produced in the favorable seasonal period of November 1 to May 1. Being invested in the market during the unfavorable seasons of May 1 to November 1 *on average* produced no additional gain.

However, those words 'on average' hide a lot of potential anguish for those who might interpret the research as saying that the market is only flat or 'dead' during its unfavorable seasons. 'On average' hides the degree by which individual years may have differed from the average.

For instance, over the 50-year period of the study, the market sometimes made gains in its unfavorable seasons. However, it was not often that those gains exceeded the interest on cash that a seasonal investor was collecting.

In the other direction, far from simply being flat or 'dead' during its unfavorable seasons, almost all of the market's serious declines, crashes, and bear markets took place during its unfavorable seasons.

Thus an investor standing aside during the market's unfavorable seasons not only matched the buy and hold performance of the S&P 500, and did so with only 50% of market risk, but also avoided the emotional stress of seeing portfolios often plunge precipitously during unfavorable seasons.

Even during bear markets most of the declines took place within the unfavorable seasons, while most bear market rallies, some of them substantial, took place during the favorable seasons.

For buy and hold investors, those unfavorable season plunges meant having to wait, sometimes for years, for the next favorable season rally, or next bull market, to bring them back to even. All the time they risked succumbing to the financial and emotional stress that could have them sell out at the lows.

Meanwhile, the seasonal investor sold out every year near the highs that were usually in place at the end of the favorable season, and bought back in the fall, usually at lower prices.

IT IS NOT A FIXED 6-MONTHS IN, 6-MONTHS OUT!

The previous research had apparently focused on monthly data, and so revealed the beginning of months, for example May 1, October 1, November 1, as key points for the annual seasonal pattern.

Our more detailed 1998 research showed very clearly that the favorable season has never been a consistent 7-month pattern, or a consistent 6-month pattern. While the favorable and unfavorable seasons last *an average* of six or seven months, they vary considerably from year to year, actually lasting between four and eight months.

That finding was very important. The time to exit was not May 1 each year. The end of the market's favorable season can be anywhere between April 20 and early July. So it could be 'Sell in April and Go Away', or even 'Sell in July and Go Away'. Likewise, the favorable season can begin anywhere between October 16 and early December.

That discovery resulted in still more research on our part, to search for a potential method of determining when the favorable season is actually beginning and ending each year.

With our expectation in 1998 that the record 1990s bull market was going to eventually end very badly, we had hope that a seasonal approach might provide a method of allowing investors to continue to participate in the powerful 1990s bull market, but also provide protection in the subsequent bear market. After all, there was the undeniable history of the market making most of its gains in the winter months, and suffering most of its serious losses in the opposite season, whether in a bull market or bear market.

The result:

How would you like an investment strategy proven by back-testing over many years, *and then in real time*, that you can learn in a half hour, that requires virtually no knowledge of how markets work (although it would be helpful), requires practically none of your time, yet produces gains that have more than doubled the performance of the Dow, S&P 500, and NASDAQ over the long-term? Keep in mind that 80% of money managers and mutual fund managers have trouble even matching the market's performance over the long-term, let alone doubling its performance.

While we're dreaming, let's throw in a couple of other attributes.

How about if this ideal strategy eliminates stock and sector risk entirely, and more than 50% of market risk?

How about if it sets you free from monitoring the market, not only on a daily or weekly basis, but was such that you'd only have to look at the market every four months or so?

What if the only 'tools' you need are the information you will be provided in this chapter, the ability to avoid 'crowd psychology', which hopefully this book will also provide you, a calendar, and a very simple technical 'indicator'?

You would probably think that such a strategy would be quite something—but could not possibly exist.

However, there is a strategy with exactly those attributes.

As noted, our 1998 research revealed that the market's favorable season varies from year to year, with its duration ranging between four and eight months. The old Wall Street maxim 'Sell in May and Go Away' was quite inaccurate.

Therefore, we (Asset Management Research Corp.) focused on finding a means by which the beginning and ending of the market's actual favorable season could be pinpointed each year with reasonable accuracy.

Not to bore you with the details of the long and time-consuming process, but through research of the previous 100 years, we established October 16 as the earliest calendar date to accept as the beginning of the market's favorable season. In the same manner, April 20 was established as the earliest calendar date to accept as the end of the favorable season each year.

After still more research we eventually found that a simple 'market-momentum-reversal' indicator, combined with those calendar dates, would provide a seasonal buy and sell 'signal'. That signal puts an investor in the market for most of the market's favorable season each year, and safely in cash for most of the unfavorable season, regardless of how long or short the seasonal periods are each year. The profit performance is remarkable.

MOVING AVERAGE CONVERGENCE DIVERGENCE INDICATOR (MACD).

The momentum-reversal indicator we chose is the Moving Average Convergence Divergence indicator, or MACD. It was developed by Gerald Appel in the 1980s, designed to signal when the market has begun either a short-term rally, or a short-term correction.

It works this way in our seasonal strategy:

If MACD is on a technical buy signal, indicating a rally is underway, when the October 16 earliest calendar date for seasonal entry arrives, we will enter at that time.

However, if the MACD indicator is on a sell signal when the October 16 calendar date arrives, indicating a market decline is underway it would not make sense to enter before that decline ends, even though the average best calendar entry date has arrived. In that event, our Seasonal Timing Strategy simply waits to enter until MACD gives its next buy signal, indicating that the decline has ended. That can be weeks, or even a month or two later, therefore sometimes significantly altering the beginning of the market's favorable season.

The strategy uses the same method to better pinpoint the *end* of the market's favorable period in the spring.

If MACD is on a sell signal when the earliest calendar exit date of April 20 arrives, we exit at that point.

However, if MACD is still on a buy signal, indicating the market is in a rally, when April 20 arrives, it makes no sense to exit the market just because the calendar date has arrived. So our Seasonal Timing Strategy's exit rule is to remain in the market until MACD triggers its next sell signal indicating the rally has ended. That can also be weeks, or even a month or two later, sometimes significantly extending the market's favorable season.

Using this strategy we are able to take advantage of the fact that the market's favorable and unfavorable seasonal periods vary significantly from year to year, sometimes being as brief as four months, other times lasting as long as eight months.

Our research into seasonality was based on the performance of the Dow Jones Industrial Average, since it was introduced at the turn of the last century making more than 100 years of data available.

The S&P 500 Index tends to move quite closely in tandem with the DJIA, since both indexes contain blue chip companies that best represent the U.S. economy at any given time. So we determined it was okay to use the signals as entry and exit signals for either the DJIA or the S&P 500.

However, we do not recommend the same strategy for the Nasdaq, since the Nasdaq tends to have a different annual seasonal pattern (more on that later).

HOW MACD WORKS.

The MACD indicator was mentioned in an earlier chapter as an example of technical 'indicators' used by market-technicians and other market-timers.

The MACD indicator consists of two moving averages, one slow moving which I show in the following charts as a dotted line, known as the trigger line, and the other faster moving, and known as the MACD line. When the MACD line, the solid line, is below the dotted trigger line, and then moves up to cross the trigger line, the indicator produces a short-term buy signal for the market. When the solid line is above the dotted trigger line, and then crosses the trigger line to the downside, a short-term sell signal is produced.

The short-term MACD indicator is a tool used by short-term traders, in that its buy and sell signals typically last from only a few weeks to as long as a month or two. Therefore it triggers many signals per year.

We use it *only* to determine whether a short-term correction is underway when the seasonal calendar entry date of October 16 arrives, which would delay the entry. And to then determine if a rally is underway when the seasonal calendar exit date of April 20 arrives, which would delay the exit. *We ignore all of the other signals that MACD produces through the year.*

The following chart shows the action of the DJIA from mid-1997 to mid-1999, which encompasses two of the market's favorable seasonal periods.

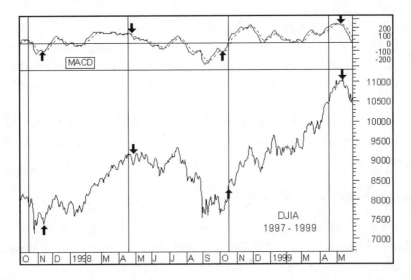

The lower window of the chart shows the DJIA itself, while the upper window shows the MACD indicator. The vertical lines are the earliest calendar entry days of October 16, and the earliest calendar exit days of April 20 the following year.

Note at the left end of the chart that when October 16, 1997 arrived MACD was on a sell signal. The entry rule of STS says we are not to enter until MACD triggers its next buy signal. As indicated by the up-arrow that did not take place until mid-November.

When April 20 of 1998 arrived, MACD was on a buy signal. The STS exit rule is that we therefore are not to exit until MACD triggers its next sell signal. In this case that took place just a few days later, and actually at a less favorable (lower) price than had we used the calendar date.

Moving on to the entry in the fall of 1998, when the earliest entry date of October 16 arrived MACD was already on a buy signal, so according to the rule we would enter at that point.

When the exit date of April 20 arrived the following spring, MACD was on a buy signal, meaning the exit would be postponed until MACD triggered its next sell signal. That did not occur until mid-May, providing almost an extra month of higher prices before STS signaled that the market's favorable seasonal period was over.

Note that MACD, like the calendar dates, does not get an investor in at the exact bottom in the fall, nor out at the exact top in the spring. No strategy could possibly do that. But MACD does provide significantly better entries and exits on average than simply using the calendar.

The important question is whether an investor following our Seasonal Timing Strategy would have matched, or perhaps beaten, the market's performance for the period. Just a glance at the chart makes the answer obvious. However, the following table provides the details.

Seasonal Timing Strategy Performance							
Entry Signal	Next-day Entry	DJIA Level	Exit Signal	Next-day Exit	DJIA Level	Profit	Compound Profit
11-14-97	11-17-97	7,698	4-23-98	4-24-98	9,064	17.7%	**17.7%**
10-16-98	10-19-98	8,466	5-10-99	5-11-99	11,026	**30.2%**	**53.2%**

Since the DJIA closed at 7,698 on 11-17-97 and at 11,026 on 5-11-99, the Dow gained 43.2% over the 18-month period. However, a 'seasonal investor' gained 17.7% in the first favorable season shown on the chart, and then sat in cash. He, or she, then made 30.2% in the next favorable season. Those two gains compounded, amount to 53.2%. To convert that to dollars, the profit on $100,000 would have been $43,200 for an investor who remained fully invested during the period, and $53,200, or 23% more, for a seasonal investor over the 18 months.

For the sake of simplicity the table shows only the profits from the DJIA price changes. A buy and hold investor would have made an additional 2.7% for the period from dividends, while the 'seasonal investor' would have made an additional 4.3% from the combination of dividends while in the market, and interest on cash when out of the market.

At the same time, market risk was significantly less for the 'seasonal investor' since he or she was in the market only 12 of the 18 months, and even then only during the less risky favorable seasonal periods.

The above chart and accompanying table also illustrate how the market's seasonal periods vary from year to year. In the first favorable period, the seasonal investor was in the market for five months, while in the second favorable period he or she was in the market for seven months.

The next chart shows the entry and exit signals on the DJIA over the nine years from 1998 through 2006, which included the final two 'bubble years' (1998 and 1999) of the powerful 1990s bull market; the severe three-year bear market that followed (2000, 2001, 2002); and several years of the new bull market that began in 2002.

Given the volatile economic and political changes that also took place during the nine years shown in the chart, it is an example of why we are able to say that the market's annual seasonal pattern is consistent through all kinds of conditions, war and peace, economic boom times and recessions, no matter which political party is in power, whether interest rates or inflation are rising or falling.

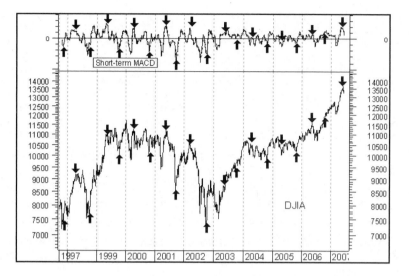

Note how the corrections in the bull markets tended to take place in the market's unfavorable seasons, while the bear market rallies during the 2000-2002 bear market tended to take place in the favorable seasons.

Also note how the 2000-2002 bear market ended, and the next bull market began almost precisely with the seasonal entry signal in October of 2002.

In the following table, the performance of the seasonal timing strategy as shown in the above chart, is converted to Dec. 31 to Dec. 31 performance each year, for easy comparison to the annual performance of the major indexes as they are reported in financial publications.

YEAR	DJIA	S&P 500	NASDAQ	STS USING DJIA Index Fund
1998 (Bull Market)	+ 17.9%	+ 28.0%	+ 39.6%	**+ 26.5%**
1999 (Bull Market)	+ 26.8%	+ 20.1%	+ 85.6%	**+ 35.1%**
2000 (Bear Market)	- 4.6%	- 9.1%	- 39.3%	**+ 2.1%**
2001 (Bear Market)	- 5.3%	-11.9%	- 21.1%	**+ 11.1%**
2002 (Bear Market)	-14.7%	- 22.1%	- 31.5%	**+ 3.1%**

2003 (Bull Market)	+ 27.6%	+ 28.7%	+ 50.0%	**+ 11.2%**
2004 (Bull Market)	+ 5.5%	+ 10.9%	+ 8.6%	**+ 8.1%**
2005 (Bull Market)	+ 1.6%	+ 4.8%	+ 1.4%	**+ 0.6%**
2006 (Bull Market)	+ 18.5%	+ 15.4%	+ 9.5%	**+ 14.2%**
9-YEAR RETURN	+ 86.3%	+ 65.5%	+ 53.7%	**+ 176.0%**
Gains are total returns, including dividends, and interest on cash when out of the market.				

The table includes 12 months of dividends each year for the buy and hold investor, dividends for the 'seasonal investor' only for the time when in the market, and interest on cash for the 'seasonal investor' when out of the market, providing the total return for each type of investor.

Does my Seasonal Timing Strategy outperform the market every year? Obviously not. As the table shows, it under-performed the major indexes significantly in 2003.

But it does consistently outperform the market in most years, and particularly when the market has a correction within the year. So that over the 9-year period shown, even though significantly under-performing in 2003, the seasonal strategy more than doubled the performance of the DJIA, almost tripled the performance of the S&P 500, and more than tripled the NASDAQ.

That performance took place in a period that incorporated not only substantial bull markets, but one of the most severe bear markets in history. In that bear market, as shown in a previous chapter on the frequency of bear markets, the DJIA lost 38.7% of its value, the S&P 500 lost 50% of its value, and the Nasdaq lost 78% of its value.

Yet our Seasonal Timing Strategy did not have a single down year. That is yet another example of how the market makes most of its gains in its favorable seasons and suffers most of its losses in its unfavorable seasons.

Was the real-time performance of our Seasonal Timing Strategy over the last 9 years an aberration? Definitely not!

The following table shows the back-tested data for the 36-year period since 1970, using the DJIA as the investment holding.

During the 36-year period when STS turned $100,000 into $10,647,516., the DJIA itself, on a buy and hold basis, including compounded dividends, would have turned $100,000 into only $5,196,284. The S&P 500, also including compounded dividends, would have turned $100,000 into only $4,752,541.

That is, the Seasonal Timing Strategy more than doubled the performance of both the DJIA and the S&P 500 over the period. So the back-testing over 36 years was almost identical to the real-time experience from 1998-2006.

Note that the largest loss suffered by the Seasonal Timing Strategy in any one year was 2.5% (in 1977). During the same period the DJIA was down 11 of the 36 years, sometimes significantly, down 16.6% (1973), 27.5% (1974), 17.2% (1977), 11.9% (2001), 22.1% (2002). And those declines from year-end to year-end do not reveal the size of some of the declines *within* some years. That is, sometimes the market suffered much more serious declines during an unfavorable season, and then recovered quite a bit by the end of the year after the next favorable season kicked in during the fall.

Once again, keep in mind that the S&P 500 is the benchmark against which professional money-manager and mutual fund performance is measured, and more than 80% fail to even match that benchmark over the long-term, let alone double it.

Our Seasonal Timing Strategy was publicly introduced in my 1999 book *Riding the Bear—How to Prosper in the Coming Bear Market*, as the strategy I recommended that would allow an investor to continue to profit in the 1990s bull market, keep those profits, and then go on to prosper further in "the coming bear market".

In *Riding the Bear* I included the back-tested data going back to 1964, based on applying the strategy to the DJIA, reporting that it had more than doubled the performance of the DJIA over that 35-year period of 1964—1999.

Yale and Jeff Hirsch reported in their newsletter, *Smart Money;*

Year	DJIA At prior year-end	STS Exit	DJIA At exit	STS Entry	DJIA At entry	DJIA Year-end	Gain/Loss Plus Interest. & Dividends	Compound Gain
								Initial Investment: $100,000
1970	800.4	4/21/1970	772.5	11/5/1970	771.6	838.9	+ 10.6%	$110,615
1971	838.9	5/3/1971	932.4	11/9/1971	837.9	890.2	+ 21.4%	$134,298
1972	890.2	4/24/1972	957.5	10/24/1972	952.5	1020.0	+ 18.7%	$159,385
1973	1020.0	4/26/1973	937.8	12/10/1973	851.1	850.9	- 2.1%	$155,995
1974	850.9	4/25/1974	827.7	10/17/1974	651.4	616.2	- 1.9%	$152,980
1975	616.2	4/30/1975	821.3	10/17/1975	832.2	852.4	+ 40.6%	$215,141
1976	852.4	4/21/1976	1011.0	10/27/1976	956.1	1004.7	+ 28.6%	$276,732
1977	1004.7	4/26/1977	915.6	10/28/1977	822.7	831.2	- 2.5%	$269,690
1978	831.2	5/8/1978	824.6	10/17/1978	866.3	805.0	- 1.3%	$266,152
1979	805.0	4/23/1979	860.1	11/2/1979	818.9	838.7	+ 17.2%	$311,894
1980	838.7	6/20/1980	869.7	10/17/1980	956.1	964.0	+ 13.6%	$354,369
1981	964.0	4/21/1981	1005.9	10/19/1981	847.1	875.0	+ 16.9%	$414,105
1982	875.0	5/3/1982	849.0	10/19/1982	1013.8	1046.5	+ 7.8%	$446,577
1983	1046.5	5/12/1983	1214.4	10/18/1983	1250.8	1258.6	+ 23.2%	$550,252
1984	1258.6	5/11/1984	1157.1	10/17/1984	1195.9	1211.6	+ 0.5%	$553,068
1985	1211.6	5/1/1985	1242.1	10/17/1985	1369.3	1546.5	+ 21.2%	$670,293
1986	1546.5	4/25/1986	1835.6	10/17/1986	1837.0	1896.0	+ 26.7%	$849,000
1987	1896.0	4/21/1987	2337.1	11/4/1987	1945.3	1938.8	+ 27.7%	$1,083,997
1988	1938.8	4/21/1988	1987.4	10/18/1988	2159.9	2168.6	+ 8.1%	$1,171,680
1989	2168.6	5/5/1989	2382.0	11/14/1989	2610.3	2753.2	+ 21.2%	$1,420,622
1990	2753.2	4/23/1990	2666.7	10/19/1990	2520.8	2633.7	+ 7.1%	$1,520,914
1991	2633.7	4/26/1991	2912.4	10/17/1991	3053.0	3168.8	+ 18.6%	$1,803,605
1992	3168.8	5/18/1992	3376.0	10/20/1992	3186.0	3031.1	+ 4.9%	$1,892,460
1993	3031.1	4/23/1993	3413.8	10/19/1993	3635.3	3754.1	+ 18.7%	$2,246,852

Year							
1994	3754.1	4/21/1994	3652.5	10/18/1994	3917.5	3834.4	-1.3%	$2,217,502
1995	3834.4	4/21/1995	4270.1	10/20/1995	4794.9	5117.1	+22.0%	$2,704,742
1996	5117.1	4/23/1996	5588.6	10/17/1996	6059.2	6448.3	+19.2%	$3,222,963
1997	6448.3	5/22/1997	7258.1	11/17/1997	7698.2	7908.3	+18.7%	$3,825,097
1998	7908.3	4/24/1998	9064.6	10/19/1998	8466.5	9181.4	+26.5%	$4,837,492
1999	9181.4	5/11/1999	11026.1	10/21/1999	10297.7	11497.1	+35.1%	$6,533,968
2000	11497.1	4/24/2000	10906.1	10/25/2000	10326.5	10786.9	+2.1%	$6,669,061
2001	10786.9	5/14/2001	10877.3	10/17/2001	9233.0	10021.5	+11.1%	$7,410,280
2002	10021.5	4/23/2002	10089.2	10/17/2002	8275.0	8341.6	+3.1%	$7,639,306
2003	8341.6	5/9/2003	8604.6	10/17/2003	9721.8	10453.9	+12.2%	$8,572,685
2004	10453.9	4/21/2004	10317.3	10/29/2004	10027.5	10783.0	+8.1%	$9,265,152
2005	10783.0	4/21/2005	10218.6	10/20/2005	10281.1	10717.5	+0.6%	$9,323,570
2006	10717.5	5/16/2006	11420.0	10/17/2006	11950.0	12474.0	+14.2%	$10,647,517.
						Total Return	+10,547%

> *"We applied Harding's system, which he developed based on the Dow's seasonal pattern, to the S&P 500. The results were astounding!" Smart Money, July, 1999*

They also included the following in their year 2000 edition of the *Stock Traders Almanac;*

> *"Tested over the last 51 years, the strategy more than doubled the already outstanding performance of our 'Best Six Months' seasonal strategy."*

Bloomberg Personal Finance Magazine reported;

> *"Remarkably simple but also remarkably profitable."*

It is said that imitation is the purest form of flattery. So it was interesting that in addition to praising my Seasonal Timing Strategy in *The Stock Traders Almanac,* and giving me full credit for developing it, Jeff and Yale Hirsch also adopted my seasonal strategy as their own. In 2000, they replaced their 'Best Six Months' strategy, which had been running in their newsletter for many years, with my Seasonal Timing Strategy, although not calling it that. When they adopted it as their own (renaming it 'Best Six Months Plus MACD') they not only began using the MACD indicator of my Seasonal Timing Strategy, but also began using the best calendar dates our research had uncovered in providing the signals.

That has caused me some embarrassing moments over the years. Since Yale Hirsch, and The Stock Traders Almanac, are so well known and widely read, when reporters interview me in relation to the market's seasonal patterns, many assume that my Seasonal Timing Strategy is actually the work of the Hirsch Organization, that *we* usurped it.

That is not the case. *Indeed, just the opposite.* The strategy came about as a result of our research showing that the market's annual seasonal pattern is *not* a six-month pattern, but varies from four to eight months.

It became even more of a problem in 2006, when Jeff Hirsch changed the credit for my strategy in their 2006 edition of Stock Traders Almanac. In my 1999 book *Riding the Bear* I called our Seasonal Timing Strategy "The Best Mechanical Strategy Ever". The 2006 edition of Stock Traders Almanac now twisted that around, saying; "Sy Harding's *Riding the Bear* dubbed trading our 'Best Six Months Switching Strategy with MACD triggers', the best mechanical system ever." For shame.

WHAT CREATES THE SEASONAL PATTERN?

Why would the market move in such consistent seasonal patterns regardless of the surrounding economic and political conditions?

The driving force is the same force that creates all market moves, a change in the amount of money flowing into the market during a specific period.

Just as the extra money that flows into the market at the end of each month creates the short-term 'monthly strength period', so significant changes take place in the amount of money that flows into the market in the fall, producing the *annual* seasonal pattern.

MONEY FLOW—THE DRIVING FORCE OF MY 'SEASONAL TIMING STRATEGY'.

As the market enters the fall season, investors begin receiving large chunks of extra cash, some of which is invested in the market automatically, with much of the rest finding its way into the market by choice.

For instance:

- Most mutual funds have fiscal years that end September 30, so they can get their books closed and make their capital gains and dividend distributions to their investors in November and December. And most investors have their mutual fund distributions tagged for automatic re-investment.

- Third and fourth quarter dividend distributions from corporations are paid to investors in the period between November and March. Most investors have their brokerage accounts tagged for automatic re-investment of dividends.

- At year-end investors begin receiving their employers' year-end contributions to their 401K and pension plans, which are usually automatically invested in the market.

- Investors receive checks from their employer's profit-sharing plans, from Christmas bonuses, year-end bonuses, from income-tax refunds in the spring, etc. Much of *those* extra chunks of money also find their way into the stock market.

- Highly paid hedge-fund managers collect their large year-end fees after the end of the year.

- Small business owners close their books at the end of each year, and once they know what their profits were for the year, distribute those profits to themselves. Much of that extra cash also finds its way into the stock market.

- Wall Street institutions, money-management firms, and knowledgeable investors, aware of the market's seasonal pattern, also begin buying more heavily, often in October, in anticipation that the market will make its usual impressive gains in the favorable season.

- Other investors, perhaps reluctant to invest in October, November, and December, still fearful after the market decline that has typically taken place during the unfavorable season, see their courage and interest return after two or three months of rising stock prices. They begin adding their money flow in January, February, March, and April.

However, in the spring that huge flow of extra money into the market dries up, with income tax refunds being pretty much the final act.

That creates a sizable decrease in money flow to fuel the market during the summer months, allowing whatever selling pressure there may be to have more influence on the direction of the market. It also deprives mutual funds and investors of the extra money needed to buy the dips, which might otherwise prevent a market decline from taking place.

Last but not least, Wall Street institutions, money-management firms, and knowledgeable investors, aware of the frequent negative effect of the market's unfavorable season, tend to take profits in the spring, as in the old adage 'Sell in May and Go Away'.

Interest in the market also diminishes by the very nature of the summer months, as many investors and traders take vacations. That can be seen in the way trading volume dries up significantly during the 'summer doldrums'.

Thus does the market almost always make most of its gains each year in the favorable seasonal period, when many billions of dollars of extra money flow in, and suffer most of its losses in the unfavorable seasonal period when that extra fuel dries up.

Seasonality is probably also the answer to the age old question of why the stock market is sometimes able to 'climb a wall of worry' (shrug off bad news), while other times it seems unable to rally even on good news. When large amounts of extra money are flowing in during the favorable season, the market tends to rally no matter that surrounding news may be negative. But when the flow of that extra 'fuel' dries up in the unfavorable season it is often difficult for the market to find enough fuel to rally even if the surrounding news is positive.

QUESTIONS.

What about the tax consequences of the annual Seasonal Timing Strategy?

Federal tax rates vary depending on an investor's tax bracket. Some states impose additional state taxes on capital gains, while others do not. Congress also changes the tax holding periods and capital gains rates fairly often. The many variables make it unworkable to back test an after-tax performance in a manner satisfactory to everyone, and impossible to predict what it would be in the future.

However, being in the market only four to eight months each year would have a tax penalty in a taxable investment account. Under current tax laws the profits each year are taxable as short-term rather than long-term capital gains. Whether that tax penalty would be serious enough to offset the benefit of more than doubling the market's performance over the long term, is questionable.

However, we *can* know that seasonal timing would have no tax impact on assets in IRAs, 401Ks, Keough plans, and other tax-deferred plans.

Nor would it have any impact on those following a strategy of making portfolio adjustments to follow changes in market leadership that usually result in holding periods of less than a year (the current threshold for long-term capital gains) anyway.

It also would not affect those who think of themselves as buy and hold investors, but on looking back at their portfolio activity realize that is not the reality, that they have engaged in a fair amount of switching in and out of holdings anyway, for one reason or another.

Seasonal timing should also have a positive impact, even considering taxes, for the majority of those who have been led to believe that since 'the market always comes back', they should simply buy and hold. It is my contention that most will bail out when losses pile up in each bear market. But unfortunately they will bail out near the market lows, rather than near the highs that are usually in place at the end of favorable seasonal periods.

Observations about taxes that are not specifically related to seasonal timing;

Using money borrowed from the government, which is what deferring taxes by not selling holdings really is, is similar to buying on margin. It leverages one's portfolio. That is wonderful on the way up, as gains are not only being made on the investor's own money, but on the money that would have been paid to the government had the holdings been sold. But, the portfolio is similarly leveraged in a down market, so declines hit investors not only on their own money, but also on that portion which is deferred taxes.

Investors also need to realize that if they're sitting on long-term capital gains on which they would pay 15% to 22% in taxes if they sold the holdings, they do not have a cushion against a market correction of 15% to 22%. If they sold they would pay the 15% to 22% tax only on that portion of their portfolio that is profit. But if they don't sell, in a market correction, a 15% to 22% decline takes place on the entire portfolio; the investor's original investment, the paper profits, and the portion that is the government's deferred taxes.

Is your Seasonal Timing Strategy valid only for the DJIA index?

The Seasonal Timing Strategy (STS) was back-tested against the DJIA because the Dow data goes back to the late 1800s. It was tested against the S&P 500 sufficiently to assume close to similar results. STS is used as one of my *Street Smart Report* newsletter portfolios in real-time utilizing index mutual funds and exchange-traded-funds (ETFs), on either the DJIA or the S&P 500. But the best results have been when used in accordance with the tested data, which was based on using the DJIA index as the holding each time.

We are not comfortable using the NASDAQ, or a sector index, to follow the signals, since they were not specifically included in the research, and have not been around long enough to necessarily provide sufficient historical data to make the research statistically meaningful.

While other holdings *might* do as well or better, it is only by using a Dow Index fund or a Dow Index ETF that we can say that if history is any guide, our STS should continue to greatly outperform the Dow, S&P 500, *and* Nasdaq over the long term.

Would the STS strategy be useful with managed mutual funds or individual stocks?

It certainly *should* be. The overall stock market, as measured by the DJIA, makes most of its gains in its favorable seasons, and as has been said about the market, 'a rising tide lifts all boats'. Most individual stocks and mutual funds therefore also make most of their gains in the market's favorable seasons (and are subject to similar risks of serious corrections and bear markets in the market's unfavorable seasons).

That said, individual stocks have a risk of their own, being subject to the changing conditions that face all companies, from the introduction of new products, rising or falling profits, the obsolescence of existing products, competition, lawsuits, and so on, that have nothing to do with the market's seasonality.

Individual managed (diversified) mutual funds were not included in the research because more than 75% of mutual funds were not in existence even 15 years ago. So there is insufficient long-term data to statistically correlate their past performance seasonally with how they might perform in the future. In addition, even if they have longer track records, a change in manager frequently changes the performance. However, that said, the market's seasonality is overpowering, and should result in their diversified portfolios following the market's seasonality to a great extent.

The goal of my Seasonal Timing Strategy is to provide investors with a simple, mechanical system that ignores 'crowd think' (which is usually bearish at good buying opportunities and bullish at market tops), does not require a lot of time, effort, or in-depth knowledge of markets or economics, yet has very high odds of outperforming the market, and therefore of outperforming the majority of mutual funds and professional money-managers. It has proven itself to do that without getting involved with individual stocks, sectors, or diversified mutual funds.

Have you considered (fill in the blank) *as a possible improvement to STS?*

After the publication of *Riding the Bear—How to Prosper in the Coming Bear Market*, we were inundated with messages from readers asking if we had looked into the use of this or that 'technical indicator' instead of MACD, or had looked into modifying the signals based on economic, political, or monetary conditions in place at the time.

The answer in general is that in the long course of our research we tried many, many variations in optimizing the strategy, including different seasonal combinations, many short-term and intermediate-term technical indicators, and modifications based on economic and monetary conditions. And what we have is the best we could find.

For instance, there are technical indicators other than MACD that have been a bit better in specific periods, but were not as consistent over the long haul. Refinements to the entry and exit signals can also be made each year by incorporating investor sentiment, overbought/oversold conditions, and support and resistance levels, rather than just MACD, and that might improve signals in some years. However, that introduces human analysis and decision-making into a strategy deliberately designed to be mechanical, specifically designed to avoid the emotional pressures of greed or fear usually involved at least to some extent in such analysis.

The goal of STS is to provide a simple mechanical strategy that any investor can utilize on his or her own. I'm not convinced that introducing complications would improve its remarkable performance. *And besides, isn't doubling or tripling the performance of the market more than enough?*

What about Wall Street firms that claim there are no seasonal patterns?

Brokerage firms and mutual fund companies would have a tough time surviving if a portion of their investors moved their money to cash for four to eight months every year. So they must go to whatever lengths they can to distort the information.

Their problem is that numbers don't lie. They are what they are.

So in trying to refute the clear proof of the market's seasonal patterns as best they can, these firms distort the data. For instance, they run the numbers from 1900, or even 1850, even though all of the research on seasonality shows the annual seasonal pattern did not begin to show up until 1950.

As noted before, the annual seasonal pattern is the result of the extra chunks of money that flow into investors' hands beginning in the fall, from mutual fund distributions, Christmas and year-end bonuses, profit-sharing bonuses, year-end contributions to 401K, IRA, and Keogh plans, income tax refunds, and so forth.

However, there were no such extra chunks of money to create favorable seasons prior to 1950. There were no mutual funds, no 401K plans, IRAs, or Keogh plans. The concept of companies sharing their profits with employees through profit-sharing plans had not yet appeared. Even income taxes were mostly non-existent in the early 1900s, and when they were introduced were a tiny fraction of what they are today.

No one who has engaged in research on the market's seasonality has ever claimed there was a significant annual seasonal pattern prior to 1950.

So when a brokerage firm runs the numbers from 1900 or 1850, and then claims the advantage of the seasonal pattern is too small to utilize, they totally distort the results they know they would have if they ran the numbers from 1950.

Further, those trying to refute seasonality invariably do not include the interest on cash that a seasonal investor would receive in the unfavorable seasons. That may not seem like much in these times. Interest rates have been as low as 1% in recent years. However, over the long-term, interest rates have sometimes been as high as 12% annually, and have averaged more than 5%. Leaving interest income out of back-testing historical data, in a market where the benchmark S&P 500 averages an annual gain of 12% over the long-term, is obviously a gross distortion of statistical analysis.

But most importantly, Wall Street's attempts to refute the market's seasonality do not tackle my Seasonal Timing Strategy, which varies the length of the favorable season from four to eight months, depending on what the market is doing at the time. *I challenge them to do so.*

The evidence is indisputable that STS has doubled and tripled the market's performance over the last 50 years. And it does so with roughly 50% of market risk.

STS did not beat the market in 2003. Does that mean seasonality has gone away?

Absolutely not! Historically there have been some individual years in which STS did not outperform the market. Those years did not prevent the remarkable 50-year record, any more than the under-performance in 2003 prevented the real-time record of the last 9 years.

In 2003 a very rare situation evolved, which actually provided more proof that it is unusual money flow that produces the market's seasonality.

Dissatisfied with the economy's slow recovery from the 2001 recession, in 2002 and 2003 the Bush Administration launched the most aggressive economic stimulus plan ever to come out of Washington. It was designed specifically to put extra money in the hands of consumers and investors. It accomplished that goal with income tax rebates, income tax cuts, cuts in capital gains taxes, and jobs creation through massive government deficit spending.

It was pointed out by critics at the time that most of the money went to the wealthiest 20% of the population, folks who did not need it as extra spending money, and so would invest it. And they did so, with the added incentive of the lowered taxes on any capital gains. Those extra chunks of money were coupled with dramatic cuts in interest rates, which made it good business for investors to also refinance mortgages and put the money into investments.

So while normally large extra chunks of money only flow into the market from October to April, in 2003 large chunks of extra money also flowed into the market during the market's unfavorable season. The result was that after rising 13% in its favorable season, the S&P 500 went on to rise an additional 15.2% in its unfavorable season when STS was out of the market in cash. So STS under-performed the market that year. Note that it did not have a loss, but only under-performed.

If anything, the market's action in its unfavorable season in 2003 provided further evidence of the dependability of seasonality, since extra chunks of money normally only flow in during the market's favorable seasons (in fact create the favorable seasons).

What is the formula for the MACD indicator?

Okay, I'll cause your eyes to glaze over by providing the formula. However, as I will explain, it is not necessary for you to know, or use it.

MACD as we use it is plotted as follows:

Using the daily closing prices of the index or security you want to plot MACD on, subtract the value of a 26-day exponential moving average of the closes, from a 12-day exponential moving average of the closes. Then plot a 9-day exponential m.a. of the indicator line, and display it on top of the solid indicator line as a dotted (or different color line), so you can tell the two apart. The dotted line is known as the trigger line.

Refer to the MACD chart shown earlier. When the solid line crosses the dotted line to the downside it produces a sell signal. When the solid line crosses the dotted line to the upside it produces a buy signal.

If you use weekly data rather than daily data, (or assuming you're doing this via computer, simply compress the daily data by a factor of 5), you will change the short term MACD indicator to an intermediate term MACD indicator. *Only the short term version is used with the Seasonal Timing System.*

However, no one plots technical indicators manually these days. Inexpensive computer software does all the work for you.

What is an exponential moving average?

An exponential moving average is calculated by applying a percentage of today's closing price to yesterday's moving average value, and doing so on a continuous basis. The idea is that by doing so, more weight is given to recent market action and increasingly less to older data.

For example, to calculate a 9% exponential m.a. of IBM: First, take today's closing price and multiply it by 9%. Then add this product to the value of yesterday's moving average multiplied by 91% (100%—9% = 91%).

M.A. = [(today's close) x 0.09] + [(yesterday's m.a.) x 0.91]

That is a very basic description. Technical analysis textbooks run to numerous pages just on moving averages.

Where can I get charting software so I can plot MACD for myself on my computer?

We use *Metastock Professional* from *Equis International, Salt Lake City, Utah*, a division of Reuters International. But, it is quite expensive, and is overkill if all you're looking for are a few simple indicators like MACD.

We have not looked into which other charting programs include MACD. However, most do. There are numerous advertisements for charting software in the advertising section of financial publications like *Investor's Business Daily*, Barron's, and Stock & Commodities magazine.

A number of free websites like BigCharts.com also allow you to plot numerous technical indicators, including MACD, with the click of a few computer keys.

(Of course I would prefer that you subscribe to my newsletter and hotline to get the signals directly from the horse's mouth as they are triggered, along with any additions or improvements that are made to the strategy as time goes by).

*Does the beginning of a favorable season guarantee there won't
be a correction before the exit signal the following spring?*

See the table of back-tested performance provided. There have
been corrections in favorable seasonal periods in the past, but they
have tended to be small and easier to hold through than the serious
corrections and crashes that mostly take place during the unfavorable seasons.

Also, keep in mind that those isolated years when losses took
place in the market's favorable seasons, or when the market continued higher in unfavorable seasons when STS was in cash, are all
included in the long-term performance data—or STS would have
had even more amazing performance.

*Are you ever tempted to deviate from the STS rules because of
current conditions?*

Oh yes, as are our subscribers, and the reason is understandable.

Seasonal timing has a strong history of getting an investor in
near important market lows, because market lows most often take
place near the end of the market's unfavorable seasons. Yet, as we
discussed in the chapter on investor sentiment, that is just the time
when surrounding economic, political, or monetary conditions
are *always* dismal and frightening. At such times, a combination
of weak economic numbers, declining corporate earnings, political uncertainties, or what have you, have usually produced a significant market decline in the unfavorable season. Thus 'the crowd'
has become increasingly gloomy by the time the low is in, and is
extending the decline in a straight line into the future, projecting
still lower prices ahead.

An investor is seeing in the media headlines, and hearing from
economists and analysts, a litany of the dismal conditions, rising
unemployment, rising interest rates, rising inflation, declining corporate earnings, preparations for war, or whatever it is that has had
the stock market in the decline. Investment newsletters as a group

are predominantly bearish. Analysts are touting all the reasons the market decline will continue.

Yet that is precisely the time when investors following our Seasonal Timing Strategy have to ignore the popular consensus, and invest.

Even *knowing* the history of the favorable season beginning in the fall, and *knowing* that conditions are always terrible at the market lows, and *knowing* that investor sentiment (the psychological crowd) is always at its most pessimistic and bearish at market lows, it is *still* difficult to go against the crowd at such times, to be willing to enter the market, particularly 100% as required by the STS rules.

So yes, we are sometimes tempted to think that "Well, maybe *this time is different*, maybe this time we shouldn't follow the STS entry signal."

Similarly, at the end of the favorable season, an impressive market rally has usually been running for four to eight months, investors are bullish, surrounding conditions look wonderful, and economists and Wall Street are euphoric and predicting the positive market will continue a lot longer without interruption. And at that time, STS requires that we ignore those conditions, ignore the bullish pressure of the crowd, take our profits, and move to cash. The concern is that we might be leaving a lot more profit on the table if the crowd is right, and based on the wonderful conditions we see when we look out the window it seems like they might be right.

So yes, it is difficult. And a couple of times over the years I have overridden the STS rules in my newsletter portfolio. For instance, by entering only 50% at what I thought was a high risk time to have an entry signal, or exiting early when the market took a scary dip in February. *Every time* it proved to be a mistake to have tried to outfox the strategy.

The Seasonal Timing Strategy gets its risk management from being in the market only 40% to 70% of the time, not from trying to second guess the strategy, or from following the crowd, or allowing the emotional feelings of greed or fear to control the decision.

SUMMING UP:

Wall Street says the market cannot be timed. But we have harnessed the very powerful annual seasonal pattern to produce an intermediate-term market-timing strategy that has a remarkable and proven track record, whether back-tested over more than 50 years, or used over the last 9 years in real time.

It not only significantly out-performs the market, but does so with 50% of market risk, since it is in the market only four to eight months a year. It also has less risk because it is only in the market in the favorable periods when the market is least likely to experience declines.

But onward.

We've covered a *short-term* monthly seasonal strategy, and an intermediate-term *annual* Seasonal Timing Strategy.

It's time to move on to a remarkably consistent longer-term market pattern, the Four-Year Presidential Cycle.

Chapter 14

The Four-Year Presidential Cycle

While most investors have at least heard of the 'Four-Year Presidential Cycle', few are aware of its particulars, or of its unusually consistent impact on the economy, the stock market, and the country's general well-being.

The cycle begins every four years at the end of each election year. Basically it is this:

- History shows a very strong tendency for the economy and stock market to experience difficulties in the first two years of each Presidential administration, and then to experience recovery and strong growth in the last two years of each term.

The driving force behind the cycle is the economic 'pump-priming' out of Washington beginning in the 2nd and 3rd year of each presidential term.

Political parties learned long ago that the most important factor for voters at election time is the condition of the economy. Regardless of how positive other factors may be at the time, almost no incumbent party has ever been re-elected if the economy is struggling when voters go to the polls.

Therefore, it has been common since at least 1918 for the incumbent Administration to do whatever it takes in the last two years of each Presidential term to make sure a prosperous economy and stock market are in place in time for the next election. Such pump-priming traditionally includes increased government spending, cuts in interest rates, tax cuts, even tax rebates. The intent is to encourage businesses to increase their capital spending and hire more workers, and to encourage consumers to spend.

It does not always work to get the incumbent party re-elected, but it almost always works to create a strong economy and stock market by the time the next election rolls around.

However, the extra stimulus efforts in the last two years of each Presidential term almost always result in the economy and stock market being pumped up *too much* when election time arrives. Excesses are created that need to be cooled off and corrected after the election. Those excesses usually include some combination of an overheated economy that is threatening to produce inflation, an overbought and over-priced stock market, perhaps a 'bubble' in one or more investment area, excess government, consumer, or corporate debt.

So after the election, the newly elected (or re-elected) Administration tends to allow the correction of those excesses to take place in the first two years of the new term. In fact, if market forces are not producing the corrections, Washington often forces the issue by raising interest rates to cool off the economy, while backing off on government spending and job creation.

It makes sense that they want the economy and stock market to undergo any needed correction of excesses in the first two years of the new term. If they tried to keep the economy and stock market pumped up for another four years, all the way to the following election, they would run the risk of even greater excesses developing. That in turn might result in an even larger economic and stock market correction late in the term, when they might not have enough time to get the situation turned around for the next election.

The risk of *not* having a market correction in the first two years of a presidential term has been demonstrated twice in the last 25 years.

The Reagan administration in its second term in the 1980s, and the Clinton administration in its second term in the 1990s, both kept the economy pumped up and booming after their re-elections. They apparently believed they could keep the economy and stock market strong all the way through their second terms, right up to the next election. However, both times the excesses in the economy and stock market became too extreme to allow that to happen.

The result for the Reagan administration was that it was hit by the 1987 stock market crash in the third year of its second term, just one year before the next election. It was an even more severe crash than the infamous 1929 crash, and raised widespread fear that it would have a similar aftermath, a long bear market and a second Great Depression. The Reagan administration did manage to get the economy and stock market recovered in time for the election the following year anyway. But it did so only by initiating dramatic cuts in interest rates, an easy money policy, and greatly increased military spending. It was a close call.

The Clinton administration was not as fortunate in its second term. It also apparently thought it could dispense with a correction of the economic and stock market excesses after its re-election in 1996. It kept the economy and stock market pumped up through the first three years of its second term. However, as would be expected, that allowed the excesses of the pre-election pump-priming to build to even greater extremes, putting the stock market into the serious 'bubble' conditions of 1999 and 2000.

The result was the bursting of the bubble early in the fourth year of the term, the election year, 2000. The bear market of 2000-2002 began when the DJIA topped out on January 14, 2000, and turned out to be the most severe since that of 1929-32. Meanwhile, the economy plunged into the 2001 recession, the Democrats lost the presidential election, and Republicans won control of both houses of Congress.

Jeremy Grantham founder and chairman of Grantham, Mayo, Van Otterloo & Co., a highly respected international manager of $140 billion in client assets, says of the Four-Year Presidential Cycle;

> *"All markets tend to drop in the first two years of a presidential cycle. The key for people to remember is that*

whoever is president has astonishingly little effect, whereas the cycle itself, the desire for the incumbent party to get re-elected, is clear in the data. . . . . The precipitating factor is economic housecleaning by officials in Washington. Presidential Administrations want to correct imbalances in the economy and smarten-up balance sheets in the first two years of their term, so they will have breathing room in year-three of the term to stimulate the economy and set things up for the next election. . . . . . An unintended consequence is that the stock market usually falls in the first two years of the cycle."

The first term of the George Bush Jr. administration is the most recent example.

The severe bear market that began on the Clinton administration's watch in 2000, continued in 2001 and 2002, the first two years of the Bush Jr. Administration. The Bush administration, following the normal cycle pattern, did little about it beyond the usual jaw-boning and rhetoric, assuring the country that "the U.S. economy is vibrant and will recover". Washington occupied itself with mending fences after the embattled and whisker-close Bush/Gore election, pushed for re-building the military, and planned for its goal of spreading democracy around the world. The terrorist attacks of September 11, 2001 came along, and further pre-occupied the Administration with the launching of the war on terror, the invasion of Afghanistan, and development of Homeland Security.

However, in the following year, the second year of the first Bush term, just as the Four-Year Presidential Cycle would have us expect, and even as the Administration could have been even more distracted by growing preparations for the invasion of Iraq, Washington moved the economy to center stage. As mentioned before, it launched the most aggressive economic stimulus effort the nation has ever seen. It increased government spending for the military and homeland security, and provided tax rebates, tax cuts, and a series of interest rate cuts that soon had mortgage and loan rates at their lowest levels in forty-five years.

Sure enough, the economy began to respond, and from its bear market low in October, 2002, the second year of President Bush's term, the stock market launched into its next bull market. Once again the stock market's Four-Year Presidential Cycle of weakness in the first two years of an Administration, and strength in the final two years, had taken place.

At the time of this writing the jury is still out on how the Bush Jr. administration's second term will play out. The pump-priming during the last two years of its first term produced the usual excesses (in stock prices, government and consumer debt, a real estate bubble, high energy costs, etc.) that would normally be corrected in the first two years of its second term. That would have been in 2005 or 2006. But it did not happen. The Federal Reserve even raised interest rates 17 times in a row beginning in 2005, in an effort to cool off the economy.

The real estate bubble did burst, and the economy did begin to slow its growth. But the stock market continued to make gains. There was no market correction in the first two years of the Bush second term.

Will that bring it trouble in the third or fourth year, as happened with the Reagan and Clinton Administrations? At this point we don't know.

THE FOUR-YEAR PRESIDENTIAL
CYCLE IN CHART FORM.

The pattern is so dependable that since at least 1918 the DJIA has made an average gain of 50% from its low in the 2nd year of each Presidential term to its high the following year. The S&P 500 has followed the same pattern since its inception.

The following chart shows the pattern over the last 18 years (four + presidential terms).

The period began with the Administration of President George Bush Sr. in 1989. The 1990 bear market took place in the 2nd year of the term. The S&P 500 lost 20.3% of its value, while the Nasdaq lost 33.8%. Then, just as called for by the Four-Year Presidential

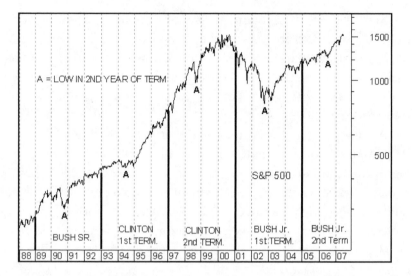

Cycle, the bear market ended with the low in the 2nd year of the term (marked A on the chart), and the market launched into a new bull market.

In the next cycle, although there was not a market decline of any degree in the first two years of President Clinton's first term, the stock market was flat for the two years. By the time of its low in 1994, marked A, the market had given back the small gain it had made in 1993. And from that low in 1994, the 2nd year of the first Clinton term, once again just as called for by the Four-Year Presidential Cycle, the market launched into a substantial multi-year up-leg.

In the next presidential cycle (Clinton's 2nd term), the market was up for both the 1st and 2nd year of the Presidential Cycle. But it did experience a serious correction in 1998, in which the S&P 500 declined 19.2%, not quite reaching the 20% decline which is the official threshold of a bear market, while the Nasdaq declined a substantial 33%. Then once again, from the low in 1998, the 2nd year of Clinton's second term, the market launched into a powerful rally, which in fact became the final two 'bubble' years of the rip-roaring 1990s bull market.

The next four-year presidential cycle began with the first two years of the first Bush Jr. administration, which was marked by the severe 2000-2002 bear market, in which the S&P 500 plunged 50%, and the Nasdaq lost 77% of its value.

And sure enough, once again the low in the 2nd year of the term was significant, marking the point where the severe 2000-2002 bear market ended, with the market launching into the new 2002-200? bull market.

In President Bush Jr.'s second term, there was no serious correction in the first two years of the term. However, from the low in the 2nd year of the term, 2006, the market did begin an impressive rally. At the time of this writing its longevity is unknown.

Let's look at the preceding four Presidential terms, in the period from 1972 to 1988:

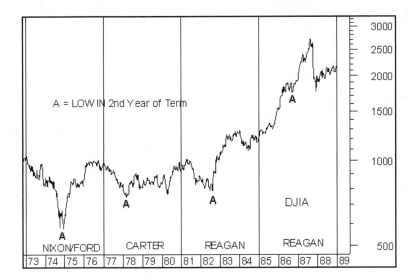

This period began with the 1973-76 presidential term, during which Gerald Ford took over the presidency after Richard Nixon resigned in August, 1974. The first two years of that presidential term saw the economy decline into the 1973-74 recession, and the stock market into the severe 1973-74 bear market. However, just as called for by the Four-Year Presidential Cycle, and just as conditions had reached an extreme of despair, the bear market ended with the low in the 2nd year of the Nixon-Ford term. From that low the market launched into a powerful new bull market, in which even the stodgy DJIA gained 75% to its high the following year. It continued to make further gains right up to the end of the next election year.

At that point the next presidential term began, that of President Jimmy Carter. All four Carter years were difficult economically, a stagnant economy and inflation that was out of control. It was an unusually brutal condition dubbed at the time as 'stagflation'. Yet even in that administration the pattern continued. The market experienced a correction in the first two years of the term, and then rallied from the low in the 2nd year to a high just after the following election.

The market continued its traditional pattern in the first Reagan term. An economic recession and a bear market in stocks took place in the first two years of the term, and the next bull market began from the low in the 2nd year.

However, as noted before, in its second term, 1985-1988, the Reagan administration demonstrated how dangerous it is to deviate from having the economy and stock market undergo corrections in the first two years of the term. The extreme excesses, particularly over-valuation of the stock market into a mini-bubble, were then corrected by the severe 1987 stock market crash that took place late in the third year of the presidential term.

With the benefit of 20-20 hindsight we now know the Reagan Administration was still able to re-stimulate the economy and stock market and have both fully recovered and looking good to voters in time for the next election at the end of 1988. However, it was a close call, with scary times immediately after the 1987 crash, the economy and stock market threatening to decline into a period that would rival the Great Depression that took place after the 1929 crash.

Yet even in Reagan's second term there was still a strong rally from the minor low at the beginning of the second year (marked A on the chart) to the high the following year (1987). And in spite of the intervening 1987 crash, an investor buying at that low would still have had a profit at the end of the next election year.

Let's go back yet *another* 16 years to the period between 1956 and 1972.

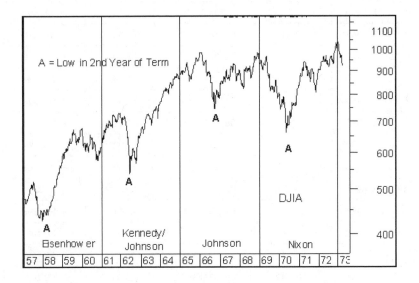

Once again note the amazing consistency with which the market suffers a serious correction in the first two years of each Administration. And note also how *every* bear market during the period ended at the low in the 2nd year of whichever Administration was in power at the time.

The previous three charts provided a pictorial tour of the amazingly consistent Four-Year Presidential Cycle over the last 50 years.

If we were to go back further, to at least 1918, the picture would be the same.

So, how does the pictorial pattern translate into real numbers?

The following table, going back 73 years to 1934, shows the actual gains of the S&P 500 from each of the 2nd year lows to the following year's highs.

LOW DATE	LEVEL OF S&P	HIGH DATE	LEVEL OF S&P	GAIN
07-26-1934	8.36	11-19-1935	13.46	+ 61.0%
03-31-1938	8.50	01-04-1939	13.23	+ 55.6%
04-28-1942	7.47	07-14-1943	12.64	+ 69.2%
10-09-1946	14.12	02-08-1947	16.20	+ 14.7%
01-03-1950	16.66	10-15-1951	23.85	+ 43.2%
01-11-1954	24.80	11-14-1955	46.41	+ 87.1%
01-02-1958	40.33	08-03-1959	60.71	+ 50.5%
06-26-1962	52.32	12-31-1963	75.02	+ 43.4%
10-07-1966	73.20	09-25-1967	97.59	+ 33.3%
05-26-1970	69.29	04-28-1971	104.77	+ 51.2%
10-03-1974	62.28	07-15-1975	95.61	+ 53.5%
03-06-1978	86.90	10-05-1979	111.27	+ 28.0%
08-12-1982	102.42	10-10-1983	172.65	+ 68.6%
01-22-1986	203.49	08-25-1987	336.77	+ 65.5%
10-11-1990	295.46	12-31-1991	417.09	+ 41.2%
04-04-1994	438.92	12-13-1995	621.69	+ 41.6%
01-09-1998	927.69	12-31-1999	1469.25	+ 58.4%
10-09-2002	776.75	12-31-2003	1111.90	+ 43.1%
06-13-06	1223.70	?—2007	?	?
			Average Gain	+ 50.5%

(Today's S&P 500, consisting of 500 stocks, was not introduced until 1957. For the years from 1934 to 1957 the performance of its forerunner, which was based on 233 stocks, is substituted in the table. Data provided by Ned Davis Research Group Inc., Atlanta, GA, and Asset Management Research Corp.).

It's important to realize that those rallies took place in *every* Four-Year Cycle, no matter which party was in power, in times of war or peace, booming economic times or bad times, rising interest rates or falling interest rates, rising inflation or declining inflation. The pump-priming beginning in the second year of each presidential term, aimed at making sure the economy is strong by the next election time *always* produced a strong stock market rally from the low in the 2nd year of the four-year cycle to the high the following year.

The dramatic variations in conditions during those 73 years included eight terms when the Republicans were in power, and ten terms when the Democrats were in power. They included periods of relative trust and admiration for the President, and periods of terrible scandals, one resulting in resignation (Nixon), another in impeachment proceedings (Clinton).

They included the assassination of a President (Kennedy), and an assassination attempt on President Reagan.

Militarily they included long periods of relative peace, but also World War II, the Korean War, Vietnam War, the collapse of communism in much of the world, the Desert Storm War, terrorist attacks, and the invasions of Afghanistan and Iraq.

Economically they included numerous recessions and numerous periods of boom times. They included periods of extremely high interest rates, in the vicinity of 15% in the 1970s, and periods of extremely low interest rates, in the Eisenhower years, and in the Clinton-Bush Jr. years, with the Fed Funds rate at just 1% in 2003.

They included periods of cheap energy costs with crude oil under $2 a barrel, and periods of high energy costs with crude oil above $70 a barrel. There were also oil embargos and Middle East wars.

There was the rise of Japan as a world power in the 1980s, and China in the 2000's.

There were periods of huge federal budget deficits, and huge federal budget surpluses.

There were periods of relative trust in corporations and Wall Street institutions, and periods of terrible scandals.

Yet through all those different conditions two situations remained constant. If there were to be any serious problems for the economy or stock market during a term, the problems almost always took place in the first two years of the term, while powerful rallies were launched from the stock market's low in the 2nd year of *every* Administration.

The Presidential Cycle is the market's main *long-term* driving force.

Economists explain economic strength or weakness, and Wall Street analysts predict the stock market's direction, by trying to interpret surrounding conditions, rising or falling interest rates, rising or falling corporate earnings and the like.

However, in the big picture, since its influence takes place regardless of surrounding events and conditions, the dominant driving force of the economy and stock market, must clearly be the Four-Year Presidential Cycle.

Obviously, the time to be extremely cautious is in the first two years of every Presidential term, and the time to buy aggressively is at the low in the second year of every Presidential term.

Chapter 15

Introducing Our Presidential Cycle Strategy

As proven in Chapter 13, our *Seasonal Timing Strategy* (based on the market's annual seasonal patterns) works extremely well using the DJIA or S&P 500 as the index holding for its favorable seasons, having more than doubled their performance over the last 50 years.

Even though its holding when in the market is an exchange-traded-fund (etf) that tracks with the conservative DJIA (or the S&P 500), its performance also beats the long-term performance of the more volatile and exciting Nasdaq.

So I am not sure why anyone would want any other strategy, or expect to find a strategy that is better.

However, individual investors still prefer to invest in Nasdaq type stocks, and are still excited by the huge gains the Nasdaq (Index) tends to make in bull markets, even though over the long-term its larger declines in bear markets tend to more than wipe out its bull market gains.

So we now introduce Street Smart Report's new *Presidential Cycle Strategy* (PCS), designed to use the Nasdaq index as the holding.

OUR PRESIDENTIAL CYCLE STRATEGY.

You are now aware of the remarkably consistent influence of politics on the stock market, in the form of the Four-Year Presidential Cycle. You are aware of the unusual buying opportunity that is presented at the low in the 2nd year of each presidential term. As shown in previous tables, since at least 1918 even the conservative Dow and S&P 500 have averaged a rally of 50% from that low in the 2nd year to their high in the following year.

However, in order to harness that power, it is obviously necessary to have a method of knowing with a fair degree of accuracy when that low has been made in the 2nd year of each cycle, and just as important to later have an exit strategy for taking the profit.

Moving Averages:

In earlier chapters we discussed the use of moving averages, which you may want to re-read since a moving average plays a big part in the strategy we have developed.

We combined the data of the Four-Year Presidential Cycle's influence on the market, and the Nasdaq's annual seasonality, with a simple 50-day moving average as the trigger line.

It provides a mechanical means of purchasing a Nasdaq Index fund reasonably near its low in the 2nd year of the Four-Year Presidential Cycle. We use the same moving average to signal an exit after the end of the following election year.

Its benefits:

- It is based on using the Nasdaq Index as the holding.

- It produces exceptional profits.

- Most of its profits will be taxed as long-term capital gains.

- It is easy to understand.

- It is mechanical in nature and so avoids 'crowd' pressures.

- It cuts market risk by approximately 40%.

- It requires making a portfolio change only twice in most four-year cycles.

The basic rules of the Presidential Cycle Strategy (PCS) are;

For the entry:

- In the 2nd year of each presidential term, enter an index fund that tracks with the Nasdaq or Nasdaq 100, on the first day *after August 15* that the Nasdaq Composite Index closes above its 50-day m.a. If the Nasdaq is already above its 50-day m.a. at the close on August 15, the entry is made the following day. *Due to the history of the Nasdaq's annual seasonality, no entry is made prior to August 15 regardless of where the 50-day moving average might be prior to August 15.*

For the exit:

- *In the year following the next election,* which would be the first year of the next Four-Year Presidential Cycle, exit on the first day *after* May 15 that the Nasdaq closes below its 50-day m.a. If the Nasdaq is already below its 50-day m.a. at the close on May 15, the exit is to be made the following day. Otherwise the exit may be delayed for several months (for as long as the Nasdaq remains above its 50-day m.a.). Once out of the market, stay out, collecting interest on cash until the entry signal the following year, which would be the 2nd year of that new term.

The results:

We'll begin by looking at the results of the strategy from the beginning of the powerful secular bull market in 1982 to the present time. If ever there was a period when market-timing would have a difficult time beating a buy and hold strategy, it would have been in that unusually long and unusually positive bull market of the 1990s.

For purposes of clarity we have broken the period beginning in 1982 down into two charts. The first chart shows the period of 1981 to 1994.

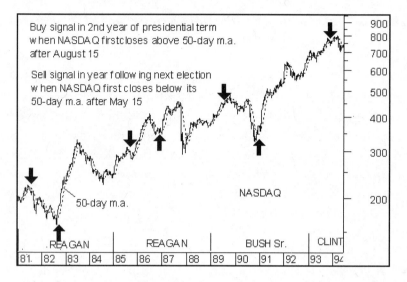

Buy signal in 2nd year of presidential term when NASDAQ first closes above 50-day m.a. after August 15

Sell signal in year following next election when NASDAQ first closes below its 50-day m.a. after May 15

The down arrows show the exits, based on the first break by the Nasdaq below its 50-day moving average after May 15 in the first year of each four-year presidential cycle. The up arrows show the entries, based on the first close by the Nasdaq above its 50-day m.a. that takes place on or after August 15 in the second year of each presidential term.

As can be seen in the chart, the strategy does not avoid all of the Nasdaq's downside volatility. While avoiding the 1981-82 bear market, and the 1989-90 bear market, an investor would still have had to hold through the 1983-84 bear market and the 1987 crash.

However, only the 1987 crash would have had a portfolio temporarily below its level at the entry signal (by 19%). The market was beginning to recover less than two months later.

The strategy did produce gains on every buy signal, including that in which the 1987 crash was involved.

The next chart shows the next period, that of 1994 to 2007.

Again in this period the strategy did not avoid all of the Nasdaq's downside volatility. In fact it would have resulted in holding through the first leg down of the 2000-2002 bear market. However, even that did not result in a losing signal, as once again each buy signal was profitable.

Yet, an investor following the strategy should have a risk-man-

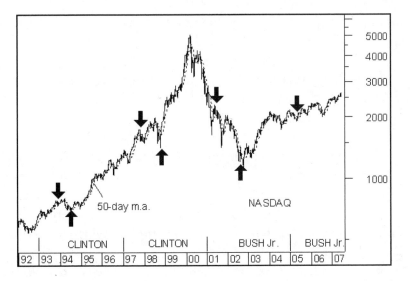

agement rule to cut such draw-downs, and I will provide that further along.

But first let's look at the results of following the strategy without use of any additional risk management.

The following table translates the above technical charts of the entire 23-year secular bull market period of 1982—2005 to a table of total return performance.

Entry Signal	Nasdaq Level	Exit Signal	Nasdaq Level	Gain	Interest When out	Gain + Interest	Compound Return.
		6-29-81	215.7				$100,000
8-23-82	172.2	8-13-85	297.6	+72.8%	+ 8.2%	+ 81%	$181,000
10-30-86	360.8	6-29-89	435.3	+20.6%	+ 8.5%	+ 29.1%	$233,671
11-12-90	352.9	7-29-93	779.3	+ 121%	+ 11.8%	+133%	$543,519
8-15-94	735.5	10-24-97	1535.1	+ 108.7	+ 3.2%	+ 112%	$1,151,717.
10-21-98	1702.6	6-14-01	2028.4	+ 19.1%	+ 5%	+ 24.1%	$1,429,280.
8-19-02	1376.6	8-24-05	2134.4	+ 55.1%	+ 1.5%	+ 56.6%	$2,238,253.

NOTE: The Nasdaq levels shown at the signals are actually its level at the close the following day. Since the signals are based on closing prices, an investor would not be able to invest on the signal until the day after it was triggered.

The strategy turned $100,000 into $2,238,253 over the period.

During the same period, the Nasdaq rose from 215.7 on June 30, 1981 to 2,134 on August 25, 2005. That would have turned $100,000 into only $989,000.

So the strategy more than doubled the performance of the Nasdaq over the period of the long secular bull market of 1982-2005.

If there were any truth at all to Wall Street's claim that the market cannot be timed, that should certainly have been a period when market-timing would not work, when simply buying and holding would be best.

So, let's go back further, into the last secular *bear* market, the type of market that causes more serious problems for investors.

A quick note on 'secular' bull and bear markets.

I'll have more to say on the subject in the next chapter on very long-term seasonal patterns. But for now suffice to say that a *secular* market is a very long-term market trend usually lasting ten to twenty years. A *cyclical* market move is a move of one to three years within the very long-term trend.

For instance, during the long 1982-2000 secular bull market there were numerous cyclical bear markets including that of 1983-84, 1987, 1990, and 1998.

In other periods the market enters long secular bear markets, in which the market goes down or sideways for many years. But within that down-trend there are numerous *cyclical* bull markets. Each cyclical bull market, while often substantial, is followed by another cyclical bear market, which keeps the market in the very long-term secular down-trend.

Our Presidential Cycle Strategy's performance in the last secular bear market:

The last 'secular' bear market ran from 1965-1982. Since the Nasdaq did not come into existence until mid-1971, we cannot know how it would have performed in the first half of that period. However, we will look at its performance in the latter half of that secular bear, after it did come into existence.

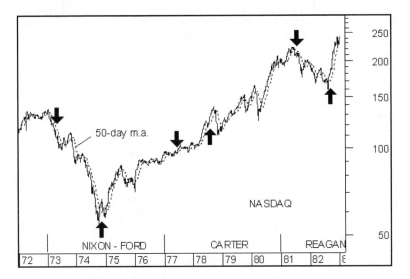

We can see at a glance that in this period the strategy also significantly out-performed being invested throughout the period, with two exits that avoided substantial Nasdaq declines (in the first two years of the Nixon-Ford Administration, and the first two years of Reagan's first term), while the two entries produced significant long-term gains.

PERFORMANCE OF OUR PRESIDENTIAL CYCLE STRATEGY SINCE THE NASDAQ'S INCEPTION:

The following table compiles the performance for the 32-year period since the Nasdaq's inception, through the strategy's most recent exit in August, 2005. That is through the latter half of a long secular bear market, through the entire next secular bull market of 1982-2000, the subsequent 3-year 2000-2002 cyclical bear market, and the first three years of the next bull market that began in 2002.

Entry Signal	Nasdaq Level	Exit Signal	Nasdaq Level	Gain	Interest When Out	Gain + Interest	Compound Return
		5-15-73	106.10				$100,000
10-14-74	61.39	5-31-77	95.86	+ 56%	+ 10.6%	+ 66.6%	$166,600.
8-15-78	132.8	6-29-81	215.75	+ 62.5%	+ 7.8%	+ 70.3%	$283,720.
8-23-82	172.2	8-13-85	297.6	+ 72.8%	+ 8.2%	+ 81.0%	$513,532.
10-30-86	360.8	6-29-89	435.3	+ 20.6%	+ 8.5%	+ 29.1%	$662,971.
11-12-90	352.9	10-29-93	779.2	+ 121%	+ 11.8%	+ 133%	$1,542,070.
8-15-94	735.5	10-24-97	1535.1	+109%	+ 3.2%	+ 112%	$3,267,646.
10-21-98	1702.6	6-14-01	2028.4	+ 19.1%	+ 5.0%	+ 24.1%	$4,055.149.
8-19-02	1376	8-24-05	2134.4	+ 55.1%	+ 1.5%	+ 56.6%	$6,350,363.

As with previous tables, the Nasdaq levels shown are its levels the day after the signals were triggered, since that would be the first opportunity an investor would have to follow the signal.

Had a 30-year old investor followed this simple strategy over the entire 32-year period, *without even trying to find something better than interest on cash when out of the market,* the investor would have turned $100,000 into $6,350,363 by the time he or she reached the age of 62.

During the same period the Nasdaq rose powerfully, from 106.1 in 1973 to 2,134 in 2005. However, that would have turned $100,000 into only $2,011,687.

So the strategy *tripled* the performance of the exciting Nasdaq itself. That does seem like ample reward for simply making just eight 'round-trip' trades over the entire 32 years.

It's also interesting to note that while one might expect such a strategy to have made most of its gains in the exciting bubble years of 1999 and 2000, it actually made its better gains in the market's troublesome years of the 1970's, early 1980's, early 1990's, and most recently from 2002 to mid-2005. What is significant about that?

First of all we will not see exciting bubble years like 1999 and 2000 very often, perhaps not again in our lifetimes, since there was only one similar period in the market's last 100 years, and that was in the late 1920s, two generations ago.

However, we are liable to experience numerous troublesome periods, since as noted in earlier chapters, the market is subjected to a cyclical bear market on average of every four years or so.

And just as important, as we will discuss in the next chapter, the odds are very high that we are now in a *secular bear market*, which began in 2000 and may last until 2020.

RISK MANAGEMENT WITHIN THE STRATEGY.

Because our new Presidential Cycle Strategy involves longer holding periods, as long as three years, there is another market pattern that can be brought into the picture to provide additional risk management.

THE MARKET'S DECENNIAL PATTERN.

The market has a very strong tendency to be negative in the 7th and 10th year of each decade. That is, years ending in 7 and 0.

The following table shows the gains and losses of each decennial year averaged over the last 120 years.

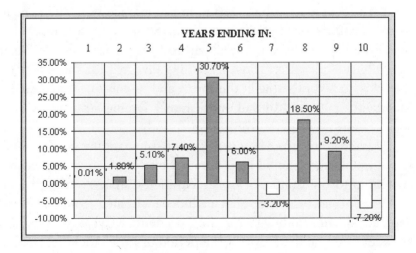

As the table shows the most positive year in each decade tends to be the 5th year. The most negative year tends to be the 10th year, while the 7th year also tends to be a down year.

The result is that over the last 120 years, if an investor had invested only in the 7th and 10th year of each decade he or she would have a loss for the effort.

That is not to say that all 7th and 10th years have been down. In fact, only 60% were down. The problem is that when they were down they were down so much, as much as 34%, that it more than offset the years that were up, producing a loss on average for the 7th and 10th years.

The most recent examples; The 1987 market crash took place in a year ending in 7, while the severe 2000-2002 bear market began in 2000. Those were also two years in our charts of the Nasdaq and our Presidential Cycle Strategy that I pointed out were difficult times for someone following the strategy, as they would have been holding through both serious declines. While doing so still produced the remarkable performance of the strategy tripling the performance of the Nasdaq over the long-term, there is a simple method of avoiding the problem.

The statistics show that over the long term it does not pay to be invested for the full year in either the 7th or 10th year of a decade.

Yet it does pay to be invested in accordance with the annual seasonal pattern of our Seasonal Timing Strategy (described in the previous chapter), even in the 7th and 10th year of each decade. That is, while the odds are against remaining invested for the full year, the odds do favor exiting in the spring and re-entering in the fall in accordance with the rules of our Seasonal Timing Strategy. In fact, that strategy avoided the 1987 crash entirely.

Therefore, to produce even greater gains and avoid potential stress, an investor should incorporate a bit of risk management by switching to our annual Seasonal Timing Strategy for the 7th and 10th year of each decade. That includes switching from the Nasdaq Index being followed for the Presidential Cycle Strategy, to an index fund on the Dow for the period of time when the annual Seasonal Timing Strategy is being used.

To look ahead a couple of decades, we would be making that risk management switch in the years 2010, 2017, 2020, 2027, and 2030.

THE PRESIDENTIAL CYCLE STRATEGY AND THE DJIA.

Our annual *Seasonal Timing Strategy* was developed for the DJIA, primarily for use in tax-deferred plans like 401Ks and IRAs, since its gains are all taxed at the higher short-term tax rates.

We have now developed the *Presidential Cycle Strategy* for those who prefer the excitement of the Nasdaq. It beats the buy and hold performance of the Nasdaq by a significant amount, *and* its profits are taxed as long-term capital gains.

CAN IT BE USED WITH THE DJIA OR S&P 500?

I know the immediate question will be whether the Presidential Cycle Strategy can also be used with the DJIA as the holding rather than using the Seasonal Timing Strategy.

The answer is; not unless you can know the market is in a secular bear market.

Over the long-term, using the DJIA as the holding in the Presidential Cycle Strategy would have achieved only half of the performance of using the strategy with the Nasdaq as the investment holding. And it would not come close to achieving the performance of our *annual* Seasonal Timing Strategy, which was designed specifically for use with the DJIA.

HOWEVER, *if* we can be sure that the 2000-2002 bear market moved us into the next long-term secular bear market, the Presidential Cycle Strategy can be modified for use with the DJIA.

The Presidential Cycle Strategy modified for the DJIA in secular bear markets only.

Most experts believe that the bear market of 2000—2002 was not just another cyclical bear market within an ongoing secular bull market, but marked a major change into the next secular bear market.

If that is the situation, then we can modify our Presidential Cycle Strategy to better suit its use with the DJIA, **but again, only for use in secular bear markets.**

For the DJIA the rule for the entry *is the same as for the Nasdaq:*

- *In the 2nd year of each presidential term,* enter an index fund that tracks with the Dow (DJIA) on the first day *after August 15* that the Dow closes above its 50-day m.a. If the Dow is already above its 50-day m.a. at the close on August 15, the entry is made the following day. No entry is to be made prior to August 15 regardless of where the 50-day moving average might be prior to August 15.

However, to exit after the next presidential election:

- *Following the election,* that is in the first year of the next Four-Year Presidential Cycle, the exit signal is triggered *on the first day of the* year that the DJIA closes below its 50-day m.a. If the DJIA is already below its 50-day m.a. when the first trading day of the year arrives, the signal is triggered that day. Otherwise the exit may be delayed for months (for as long as the DJIA remains above its 50-day m.a.).

Let's take a look at how investing in the Dow in accordance with this modified Presidential Cycle Strategy would have worked in the last secular bear market of 1965-1982. The period encompasses five presidential terms. In order to make the charts more legible we will break the period down into two charts.

The first chart shows the entries and exits of the Presidential-Cycle Strategy (modified for the DJIA), in the eight years between 1965 and 1972.

During this period the market produced considerable emotional

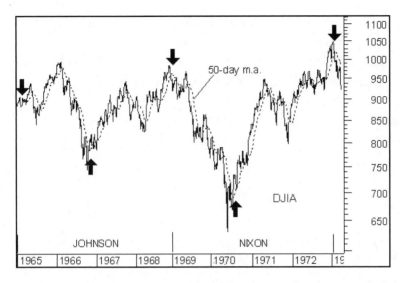

and financial pain for a buy and hold investor. The Dow ended the 8-year period virtually at the same level where it began. But it experienced declines of as much as 40% on the journey.

However, the Presidential Cycle Strategy was obviously superb in avoiding the serious corrections and bear markets, while catching most of the gains of the two substantial bull markets.

The next chart completes the last secular bear market period by showing the entry and exit signals for the strategy between 1972

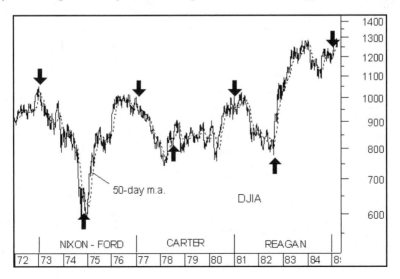

and 1982 (and to the end of the Four-Year Presidential Cycle of the first Reagan term).

In this period the advantage of the Presidential Cycle Strategy in out-performing the market is also obvious.

The results of following our Presidential Cycle Strategy for the entire 20-year secular bear market depicted in the previous two charts, are shown in the following table.

Entry Signal	DJIA Level	Exit Signal	DJIA Level	Gain	Dividends + Interest	Total Return	Compound Return
		1-4-65	875.9				$100,000.
10-18-66	785.4	1-2-68	951.9	+21.2%	11.5%	+ 32.7%	$132,700.
8-15-70	709.1	1-22-73	1018.7	+ 43.7%	21.3%	+ 65.0%	$218,955.
10-21-74	662.9	1-18-77	968.7	+ 46.1%	25.9%	+ 72.0%	$376,603.
8-15-78	894.6	1-20-81	946.2	+ 5.7%	23.9%	+ 29.6%	$488,077.
8-17-82	829.4	1-2-85	1189.8	+43.4%	34.8%	+ 78.2%	$869,753.

Notes: The 'DJIA Levels' in the table are as of the close the day following the entry or exit signal. (Since the signals are based on the market's close, an investor would not be able to follow the signal until the following day).

Dividends and interest shown are the totals for the period when in or out after each signal.

The strategy produced a total compounded return of 769.7% over the entire secular bear market. By comparison the DJIA began 1965 at 874.1 and closed on December 31, 1982 at 1,046.5. It therefore gained a total of only 19.7% *over the entire 20-years.*

However, a buy and hold investor would also have collected dividends. Based on those dividends having been re-invested each year, the total compounded return of the DJIA over the 20-year period would have been 164%, and would have turned $100,000 into $264,222.

So modified for the Dow, the Presidential Cycle Strategy more than tripled the performance of the Dow during the period of the secular bear market of 1965-1982, and achieved that remarkable market-timing by making just five round-trip trades over the 20 years, a small effort for an investor to make for such a large difference in profits.

It did so by making the gains (and the dividends) in the market's big rallies from the low in the 2nd year of each presidential cycle to the end of the next election year, and then being out of the market collecting interest on cash during the market declines that frequently take place sometime in the first or second year of each term.

In addition to the substantially larger profits, the strategy was in the market only 140 months, or 58% of the time, and safely in cash for a total of 100 months. Thus the strategy more than tripled the performance of the market while taking only 58% of the market risk an investor would undertake by being in the market 100% of the time.

However, as pointed out, this modified version of the strategy works for the Dow only in secular bear markets.

Over the long-term, through secular bull and secular bear markets, our Seasonal Timing Strategy has by far the best record for use with the DJIA, while our new Presidential Cycle Strategy has the best record for use with the Nasdaq.

Investors using either our proven Seasonal Timing Strategy with the DJIA, or our new Presidential Cycle Strategy with the Nasdaq, should significantly out-perform the market over the long-term, with considerably less market risk.

How great is that?

Consider that, as I pointed out earlier, over the long-term more than 80% of mutual funds fail to even *match* the performance of the S&P 500 index.

Then consider, as we also discussed in previous chapters, that even those mutual funds that do outperform for a few years, are rarely able to continue that performance over the next few years, let alone over the long-term.

What if we use leverage with the seasonal market-timing strategies?

The exceptional performance figures shown for our *Seasonal Timing Strategy*, and our new *Presidential Cycle Strategy*, were achieved by using DJIA and Nasdaq indexes without leverage.

Strategies that double and triple the market over the long-term, with less than market-risk, *should* satisfy anyone, including money-managers, financial institutions, and their clients.

However, if an investor utilized leveraged positions when following the entry and exit signals the market-beating performance should be even more remarkable.

The introduction in recent years of leveraged index mutual funds, and leveraged index exchange-traded-funds (ETFs) provide investors these days with easier methods of obtaining leverage than were possible in previous periods, when buying on margin was about the only way to achieve leverage.

Funds are now available that leverage the performance of the specific indexes for which our strategies were designed, that is the DJIA, S&P 500, and Nasdaq. Depending on the fund chosen, the leverage can vary from 1.5 to 1 (which means the fund is designed to move one and half times as much as the underlying index), to leverage of 2.5 to 1 (meaning the fund is designed to move two and half times as much as the index).

Just keep in mind that leverage applies in both directions. A fund that is leveraged to move up twice as much as the underlying index moves up, will also move down twice as much as the underlying index moves down on those occasions when the market does not move as expected.

That will double the volatility one will experience in following a long-term strategy. It will also increase the potential for an investor to give up on a long-term strategy in short-term periods when the strategy doesn't seem to be working.

The most popular fund families providing leveraged mutual funds are:

Rydex Series Funds,
9601 Blackwell Road
Rockville, Maryland, 20850
1-800-820-0888
www.rydexfunds.com

Profunds
c/o BisysFund Services
3435 Stelzer Road,
Columbus, OH 43219-8001
1-888-776-3637
www.profunds.com

Direxion Funds
c/o U.S. Bancorp Mutual Funds Services
P.O. 0701
Milwaukee, WI 53201
1-800-851-0511
www.direcionfunds.com

LEVERAGED EXCHANGE TRADED INDEX FUNDS (ETFS).

As mentioned in a previous chapter a number of leveraged exchange-traded-funds are also available, designed to move twice as much as the index moves.

Some of those include:

Ultra QQQ, symbol QLD. Leveraged 2:1 to the Nasdaq 100 Index.

Ultra S&P 500, symbol SSO. Leveraged 2:1 to the S&P 500 Index.

Ultra Dow 30, symbol DDM. Leveraged 2:1 to the DJIA (Dow).

FURTHER OPTIMIZING OF THE STRATEGIES.

As remarkable as the seasonal and cycle strategies are, they can sometimes be optimized in individual years through analysis of technical conditions at the time. Downside positioning in short-sales or bear-type mutual funds can work out in some unfavorable seasons when technical analysis is showing the market to be at particular risk of a sizable downturn.

However, since those conditions will be different each year, and can only be incorporated at the time, they are best left to experienced market technicians (or the on-going market analysis provided in market-timing newsletters).

However, the exceptional performances shown for our strategies were achieved by mechanically following the simple 'rules' of each strategy without any additional input, and employing only cash in the 'unfavorable' seasons.

Chapter 16

The Very Long-Term Market Patterns

We've discussed very short-term intra-day trading patterns. They are of value mostly to day-traders.

We covered the Monthly Seasonal Strategy developed by Norman Fosback, and its exceptional performance by trading in and out of the market for its strongest periods each month.

We covered my *annual* Seasonal Timing Strategy, which harnesses the remarkable consistency of the market's favorable and unfavorable seasons each year. It has more than doubled the performance of the DJIA, S&P 500, and NASDAQ over the long-term, and requires just two trades per year.

We covered my new Presidential-Cycle Strategy, which harnesses the consistency of the Four-Year Presidential Cycle, and requires just two trades in each four-year period.

There is yet another even longer-term consistent pattern that we should discuss.

We do not have a separate strategy for handling it, (my annual Seasonal Timing Strategy for the DJIA, and Presidential Cycle Strategy for the NASDAQ, worked well through these long-term patterns), but I believe it is important that all investors be aware of the pattern.

CYCLICAL AND SECULAR MARKETS

As noted briefly in previous chapters, a *secular* market is a very long-term market trend usually lasting ten to twenty years. A *cycli-*

cal market move is a move of one to three years within that very long-term trend.

For *at least* the last 100 years the market has cycled back and forth between these secular bull and secular bear market periods every 10 to 20 years, with secular bear markets tending to last longer than secular bull markets. If data was available for the 1800s we would probably see the same pattern.

Basically, the last hundred years can be divided into six periods:

1901-21: 20 years of a sideways to down secular bear market.

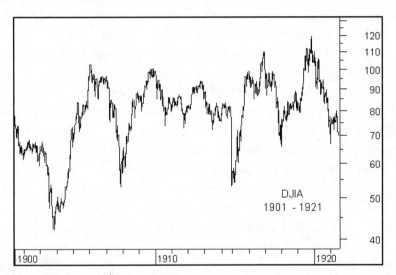

DJIA
1901 - 1921

As the chart shows, the market went nowhere on a buy and hold basis for the entire 20-year period from 1901 to 1921, a classic secular (very long-term) bear market. It ended the period essentially where it began, at approximately 75 on the Dow.

Expressed that way, as a market that ended where it began, it sounds at least like a flat and easy period to hold through, even if profitless.

However, as the chart shows, it was far from that. There were five substantial cyclical bear-markets within the long-term secular trend, or one on average of every four years, and four cyclical bull markets. The combination kept the market in the long-term flat sideways trend. Meanwhile, the up and down volatility made it a terribly stressful time for buy and hold investors, with declines up to 50% even for the conservative Dow.

However, I'm sure there were few if any buy and hold investors still holding after even 10 years of such stress, let alone 20 years of it. Market-timing and intermediate-term trading was the only acceptable strategy of successful investors. The big-names of the time; Joseph P. Kennedy, Walter Chrysler, Bernard Baruch, Vanderbilt, J.P. Morgan, and hundreds of others, became extremely wealthy taking profits as bull markets became over-extended, buying back at the low prices after a decline, and even selling short near the tops to make additional gains from the downside.

That period was followed by:

1921-29: Eight Years of a very strong secular bull market.

During this period the market, as measured by the Dow, averaged 25% gains per year for eight years. The most serious corrections did not even qualify as cyclical bear markets, the definition of which is a decline of 20% or more. There was a 19.5% decline in 1921, a 19% decline in 1923, and a 16% decline in 1926.

It was a record length of time without a bear market, causing investors to finally adopt a buy and hold approach again.

In fact, beginning in 1928 investors became unusually confident and euphoric, convinced they were in a new era in which the good times could go on forever. They bought almost in a frenzy, at ever higher prices, without regard to valuation or other normal investment considerations, driving the market into a rare and dangerous 'bubble'.

When the 'bubble' broke in 1929, that super bullish secular bull market was followed by:

<u>*1929-49: Another 20-year secular bear market.*</u>

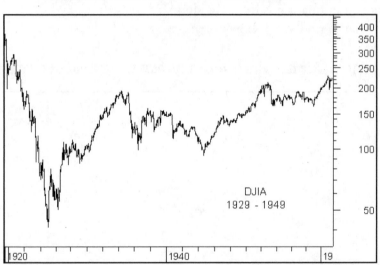

This secular bear market began when the 1929 market bubble burst with a severe one-day crash, the infamous '1929 Crash'. It continued down in a frightening cyclical bear market that lasted until 1932. By that time, the Dow had lost 90% of its value.

During the entire 20-year period of 1929-1949, the market remained well below its levels of 1928 and 1929.

But it was another great time for market-timers. There were six cyclical bear markets in those 20 years, and five cyclical bull markets.

Except for the initial plunge from the 1929 high, they do not look like much in this chart, due to the distortion of that initial plunge. However, the cyclical bull markets during the period produced gains for the Dow ranging from 50% to 125%.

Each was followed by a cyclical bear market in which the losses were as much as 49%. So, overall, the market moved sideways for the entire period. In fact, it is not shown on the chart, but as shown in earlier chapters, the market did not get back to its 1929 level for 26 years. *And in order to even achieve that recovery, most of the stocks that made up that index had been replaced with stronger stocks.*

That secular bear market was followed by:

1949-66: 17 years of the next secular bull market.

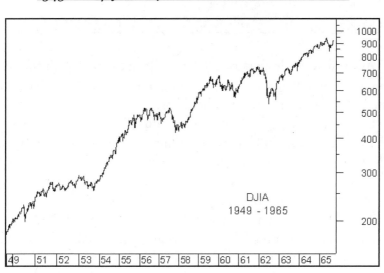

DJIA
1949 - 1965

The DJIA averaged annual gains of 14% per year over this 17-year period.

However once again, within the long secular bull market there were substantial corrections, and cyclical bear markets. The declines were as much as 26%.

That 17-year secular bull market was followed by:

1966-1982: 16 years of the next secular bear market.

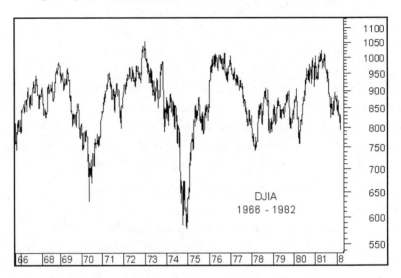

DJIA
1966 - 1982

Again it was a long period (16 years) that ended with the market right where it was at the beginning of the period, producing no gain, but no loss on a buy and hold basis.

However, although the market produced virtually no gain over the 16 years, it was still a period when by far the majority of investors and money managers failed to match even its flat performance. There were just too many serious corrections and bear markets that create problems for normal portfolio management.

The DJIA reached 1000 for the first time in 1966. Over the next 16 years it climbed back up to and fractionally above 1000 numerous times in cyclical bull markets, only to plunge back down each time. It did not exceed that level and continue higher until 1982 when the next secular bull market began.

It was another difficult time for buy and hold investors, another wonderful time for market-timers who followed strategies, like seasonal strategies, that got them in for most of the bull markets, and out for most of the bear markets.

That 16-year secular bear market was then followed by:

1982-2000: 18 years of a very strong secular bull market.

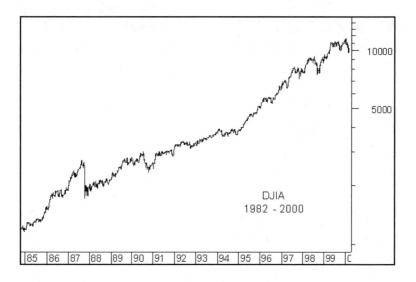

During the period there were cyclical bear markets, including the 1987 crash, the 1990 cyclical bear market, and a decline in 1998 of 33% for the Nasdaq. But by and large, it was a long period of rising market, particularly from 1991 on.

Beginning in 1995, as had happened in the late 1920's, the long period without a serious correction made investors extremely confident and euphoric, convinced they were in a new era in which the good times would go on forever.

As they did in 1928 and 1929, investors bought almost in a frenzy in 1998 and 1999, at ever higher prices, without regard to valuation or other normal investment considerations. In the process, just as in the late 1920s, the market was driven into a rare and dangerous 'bubble'.

When the 'bubble' broke, that long secular bull market was followed by:

The severe 2000-2002 cyclical bear market, and a subsequent cyclical bull market.

In the next chart I have shown the Nasdaq as representative of that bear market, and subsequent bull market, since in the previous bull market, and particularly in its final bubble years, the Nasdaq had become the favorite investment area for investors.

In the 2000-2002 cyclical bear market, the Nasdaq lost 78% of its value. In the subsequent cyclical bull market it has recovered roughly only half of its loss.

As I pointed out in my 1999 book *Riding the Bear—How to Prosper in the Coming Bear Market*, the Nasdaq's final bubble years were eerily similar to the final bubble years of the Dow in the late 1920s. And as I expected, it turned out that the Nasdaq's subsequent three-year bear market of 2000-2002 was just as eerily similar to the serious three-year bear market of 1929-32.

That seven years have now gone by since its 2000 peak, and the Nasdaq has been able to recover only half of its bear market losses, is also uncomfortably similar to the beginning of the long secular bear market that followed the 1920-1929 secular bull market.

That begs the question;

Did the next long *secular* bear market begin with the 2000-2002 cyclical bear market?

That is a very important question for investors going forward.

Obviously from the history of secular bear markets shown in this chapter's charts, secular bear markets are wonderful times for market-timers, but terrible times for those who get caught up in the thought that bull markets run forever.

As the severity of the 2000-2002 bear market unfolded, market analysts, even Wall Street experts, pretty much agreed that it was indeed the beginning of the next 17 to 20 year secular bear market.

Even perpetually bullish Wall Street firms were warning investors, "We are now in a secular bear market. Investors should expect profits from the market to *average* no more than 5 or 6% per year for the next 10 to 15 years. There will be big cyclical bull markets. But they will be followed by cyclical bear markets that take most of the gains back."

Most of the world's famously successful investors agreed. Warren Buffett warned in numerous interviews in 2002, and letters to his investors, that "the next 17 years will be unlike the last 17 years".

If we were looking *only* at the chart of the Nasdaq, it would be difficult to argue that we are not in the early stages of the next secular bear market.

A chart of the S&P 500 does not completely disabuse me of that thought.

The S&P 500 has regained much more of its losses than the Nasdaq has managed since the 2000-2002 bear market ended. But yet, it has taken seven years for the S&P 500 to recover to its level of 2000. So now the question as this is being written in mid-May, is whether it will be able to continue rising to new all-time highs, or will endure a cyclical bear market that takes back some of the gains of the bull market that began in 2002, and keeps the S&P below its peak level of 2000.

The picture is even more foggy when we look at the Dow's performance since the 2000-2002 cyclical bear market ended.

In the 'new' cyclical bull market that began in 2002 the DJIA has recovered all the way back to its bull market peak of early 2000, and gone on to higher highs that have the DJIA 15% above its level at its peak in 2000.

Other market indexes, including the DJ Transportation Average and DJ Utilities Average have similarly climbed back above their levels at the bull market peak in 2000.

So it is a mixed picture whether or not the 2000-2002 bear

market was a cyclical bear market or the beginning of a long secular bear market as so many believed at the time.

What we can know.

We can know that the seasonal timing strategies outlined in this book have worked well to outperform the market over the long-term in both secular bull and secular bear markets.

Therefore if we follow one of those seasonal strategies we should not have to be concerned about surrounding conditions, cyclical bull or bear markets, or secular bull and bear markets.

Happy investing!

Addendum

What have we learned?

- The market cycles between bull and bear markets much more frequently than most investors realize, with a bear market arriving on average of every 4 years. Having a strategy that deals with them is of vital importance.

- Buy and hold investing is a badly flawed theory that contributes to the record of most investors buying high and selling low.

- Wall Street institutions, mutual fund managers, money-management firms, corporate insiders, and large private investors, who advise public investors to simply buy & hold, do not buy & hold with their own money.

- The financial media rarely provides a balanced picture since they depend on Wall Street for their information.

- The playing field is decidedly tilted against public investors.

- Individual investors do not have the training or facilities to compete head to head with professional money management firms, and need a strategy that works without such requirements.

- Trading on 'tips', or chasing the previous year's winners, be they mutual funds or individual stocks, is bad strategy.

- Avoiding the influence of the 'psychological crowd' is of utmost importance.

- Wall Street is dead wrong and totally misleading when it claims the market cannot be timed. Its institutions and professional players all engage in significant market-timing, of individual stocks and the overall market.

- The market moves in clear seasonal movements, monthly, annually, and in four-year cycles, and for understandable reasons that will not change.

- Those seasonal movements can be harnessed to provide market-beating performance that allows investors to compete very successfully against the professionals, without need for professional training, data, or facilities, and with only 50% of market risk.

- A seasonal strategy will be even more important if we are in secular bear market.

  Again, happy investing!

Glossary of Important Investment Terms

Insiders. These are the people in a position to have inside information about a company that could affect the stock price if the information were known to other (outside) investors. They include directors, senior officers, and top management. A person or entity that owns greater than 10% of the voting shares of a corporation is also considered an insider under the law.

Insider Trading. This the buying and selling of their shares by company insiders. Insiders are required to report their trades in a timely manner. It is considered to be useful information to know if insiders are buying or selling the shares of their company to any unusual degree.

Margin. Buying on margin is a form of leverage. Investors use money borrowed from their brokerage firm for part of the purchase price, paying interest on the loan. Margin terms depend on the type of transaction. Generally, an investor can margin 50% of the purchase price of most individual stocks.

Margin Account. In order to use margin an investor must open a margin account with his or her brokerage firm, and agree to its terms.

Margin Call. If the value of a stock declines to less than its purchase price after it has been purchased on margin, the investor's equity in the stock may no longer equal 50% of the value of the stock. Brokerage firms allow only so much slippage, and then will issue a 'margin call', which is a demand that the investor send in more money to bring the account back up to margin requirements. If the investor fails to do so the brokerage firm can sell all or part of the stock to recover the money it loaned.

Market Cap. This refers to a market's 'capitalization'. It is simply the value at the moment of all the company's issued and outstanding shares, at the current selling price of the shares.

Market-maker. Market-makers are the licensed brokerage firms who facilitate the trading in particular stocks. By agreeing to buy or sell certain stocks a market-maker provides a ready market by which investors can make their trades. Market-makers make their profit on the 'spread', which is the difference between the bid price (the price at which they will buy) and the ask price (the price at which they will sell).

Market Order. An 'at the market' order is an order an investor places to be executed at the current market price. That is, a 'market order' to buy will be executed at the market-maker's current 'ask' price. A 'market order' to sell will be executed at the market-maker's current 'bid' price.

Limit Order. A 'limit order' is an order that limits the price at which the market-maker can execute the trade. This prevents an order from being executed at a price quite different from what the investor is willing to accept.

Price/Earnings (P/E ratio). A stock's P/E ratio is the stock's price divided by the company's earnings per share. It is a method of measuring a stock's value. A *projected* P/E ratio divides the current share price by the earnings it is estimated a company will have in the future, usually over the next four quarters.

Overhead Resistance. This is a level that a stock, mutual fund, or market index, may have a difficult time rising above. It might be a level where previous rallies have failed, or a level where it is over-extended (overbought) above an important moving average, or an area where a trendline can be drawn through its previous highs.

Support Level. This is a level where a declining stock, mutual fund, or market index, may find 'support'. That is a point where buying is likely to come in and end the decline. It might be a level where previous declines have ended, or a level where it is over-extended (oversold) beneath an important moving average, or an area where a trendline can be drawn through its previous correction bottoms.

Short Sale. 'Selling short' refers to borrowing a stock from one's broker, and selling it at the current price. At some point the short-seller must buy the stock (hopefully at a lower price) and return the borrowed shares to the broker to close the position out. For example, if an investor believes IBM shares are going to decline in price, the investor could sell the stock short, receiving the present price of IBM. If IBM does decline in price the investor then buys IBM shares at the lower price to replace the shares borrowed from the broker. Since the investor has sold high and then bought low, the difference is profit. Obviously if IBM moves higher rather then lower, the investor will have a loss on the short position when it is closed out. An investor must have a margin account, and the brokerage firm's permission to sell short, and pays the brokerage firm interest on the value of the borrowed stock until the position is closed.

Volatility. The measurement of how much a stock, mutual fund, or market fluctuates in price over a period of time. It is volatility that provides the profits or losses that an investor will experience, and the risk that is involved.

About the Author

Sy Harding began his career in engineering, rising quickly (in his mid-twenties) to the position of chief engineer, and then vice-president, of a manufacturing company in the lakes region of New Hampshire.

He left that company to launch a high-tech manufacturing company, Cametrics Inc., in Connecticut, which he subsequently built to substantial size and sold to a Wall Street firm.

Harding then launched another high-tech manufacturing company, this time in New Hampshire. He built this company to substantial size and sold to a publicly traded company.

Harding then founded Asset Management Research Corporation, for the purpose of providing stock market and economic research to institutions and serious investors. Harding's engineering background, coupled with the experience of operating businesses through numerous economic cycles, made it natural that a good portion of the research involves technical analysis and charting of markets, as well as analysis of the economic fundamentals that affect markets.

The firm has been publishing its research for the public for more than 20 years, at first in the form of *Sy Harding's Street Smart Report*, a newsletter, and since 1997 as Street Smart Report Online on its website www.StreetSmartReport.com.

Harding is frequently ranked highly in the 'Top Ten Market Timers in the U.S.', and is quoted frequently in the financial media.

He lives in Florida with his wife Dale.

If you would like to be notified when Sy Harding's next book

'Being Street Smart' is available, please provide contact information below and mail to:

Asset Management Research Corp.
505 East New York Ave., Suite 9
DeLand, FL 32724.

Name. . . . .
Street Address. . . . .
. . . .
City, State, Zip Code. . . . .
e-mail Address . . . .

- Don't worry! We do not sell or rent mailing lists. Your information will be used only by us, and only to contact you with information you request.

If you would like to buy a copy of *Beat the Market the Easy Way* for a friend we would be pleased to mail it direct for you. Contact Asset Management Research Corp.

Money Managers, Financial Advisors, & Institutions:

'Beat the Market the Easy Way' is available at quantity discounts, as few as 5 copies. Contact Asset Management Research Corp.

Subscribe to Sy's online newsletter and website!
Sy Harding's Street Smart Report Online!

Home of:

Seasonal Timing Strategy
&
Presidential Cycle Strategy

20 years of exceptional research for serious investors!

The newsletter is published online for your print-out every three weeks! There is a mid-week update on the economy, stock market, bonds, and gold every Wednesday! An online hotline is provided when signals or recommendations change! There is a weekly 'Being Street Smart' column, access to 'Street Smart School' for articles on chart reading and technical analysis, and lots more!

$225 1 year. (The cost of two cups of coffee per week)
$350 2 years.
$21.95 monthly (By automatic monthly credit card payment).

Mail check to;
Asset Management Research Corp.
505 East New York Ave., Suite 9,
DeLand, FL 32724

For faster service subscribe online at;
www.StreetSmartReport.com OR;
Call the subscription office at 1-386-943-4081.
We honor all major credit cards.

Sy's Timer Digest Rankings:

1990: #2 Stock Market Timer in the U.S.
1991: #2 Long Term Market Timer.
1991: #1 Gold Timer (Gold Timer of the Year).
1992: #1 Gold Timer Two Year period.
1992: #1 Stock Market Timer 3 Year period.
1993: #1 Gold Timer 3 Year period.
1993: #2 Long Term Stock Market Timer 3 Yr Prd.
1994: #5 Gold Timer last 12 months, May 16.
1998: #10 Stock Market Timer in U.S.
1999: #2 Bond Market Timer last 12 months. July, 1999
1999: #4 Gold Timer last 12 months. Sept 1999.
1999: #3 Stock Market Timer last 6 months. Dec., 1999
2000: #3 Stock Market Timer last 6 months. Jan., 2000.
2001: #3 Bond Timer last 12 months. Sept. 2001.
2001: #7 Stock Market Timer for 2001
2002: #3 Gold timer last 12 months. Mar. 2002
2002: #3 Stock Market Timer last 12 months. July, 2002
2003: #4 Stock Market Timer last 3 months. Aug, 2003.
2003: #1 Gold Timer last 12 months, Sept. 2003
2004: #2 Gold Timer last 12 months, Feb., 2004.
2004: #9 Stock Market Timer last 3 months. May, 2004.
2004: #5 Bond Timer for 2004.
2005: #2 Gold Timer last 12 months. Nov., 2005.
2006: #5 Bond Timer last 12 months. Dec., 2006.